Teaching Digital Kindness

Digital tools have a clear educational purpose, but how do we help students with the darker corners of the web? This book provides timely, much-needed advice for educators on how to teach students to handle the anger and divisiveness that pervades social media and that is impossible to ignore when using tech for other purposes.

Author Andrew Marcinek provides strategies we can use to help students with issues such as navigating relationships; understanding digital ethics and norms; returning to a balance with screen time; reclaiming conversation; holding yourself accountable; creating a new digital mindset; and more.

Throughout, there are practical features such as Pause and Reflects, Teachable Moments, and classroom activities and lesson plans, so you can easily implement the ideas across content areas and grade levels.

Andrew Marcinek serves as the Chief Digital Learning Officer at Buckingham Browne & Nichols School in Massachusetts. He was the first Open Education Advisor at the United States Department of Education before joining BB&N. He has also worked as a teacher and administrator in both the private sector and public education.

T0373665

Also Available from Routledge Eye On Education

www.routledge.com/k-12

Close Reading the Media:
Literacy Lessons and Activities for Every
Month of the School Year
Frank Baker

The Media-Savvy Middle School Classroom:
Strategies for Teaching Against Disinformation
Susan Brooks-Young

Building Transformational Kindness in Schools:
A Guide for Teachers and Leaders
Hope E. Wilson

Teaching Digital Kindness

Helping Students Become More Aware and Accountable in Their Online Lives

Andrew Marcinek

Routledge
Taylor & Francis Group

NEW YORK AND LONDON

Designed cover image: © Getty Images

First published 2024
by Routledge
605 Third Avenue, New York, NY 10158

and by Routledge
4 Park Square, Milton Park, Abingdon, Oxon, OX14 4RN

Routledge is an imprint of the Taylor & Francis Group, an informa business

Library of Congress Cataloging-in-Publication Data
Names: Marcinek, Andrew P., author.
Title: Teaching digital kindness: helping students become more
aware and accountable in their online lives / Andrew Marcinek.
Description: New York, NY: Routledge, 2023. |
Series: Routledge eye on education |
Identifiers: LCCN 2022060866 | ISBN 9781032281544 (paperback) |
ISBN 9781032293721 (hardback) | ISBN 9781003301325 (ebook)
Subjects: LCSH: Social media—Moral and ethical aspects. |
Interpersonal communication—Moral and ethical aspects.
Classification: LCC HM742 .M3527 2023 |
DDC 302.23/1071—dc23/eng/20230411
LC record available at https://lccn.loc.gov/2022060866

ISBN: 978-1-032-29372-1 (hbk)
ISBN: 978-1-032-28154-4 (pbk)
ISBN: 978-1-003-30132-5 (ebk)

DOI: 10.4324/9781003301325

Typeset in Palatino
by codeMantra

For my wife Caroline and our future children

Contents

Meet the Author

In Cambridge, Massachusetts, **Andrew Marcinek** serves as the Digital Learning Officer at Buckingham Browne & Nichols School. Andrew was the first Open Education Advisor at the United States Department of Education before joining BB&N. While at the Department of Education, Andrew worked to increase the speed at which open education policies were adopted; he also advocated for the federal government as a whole to adopt more open education policies and backed efforts to increase the amount of open educational materials curated and shared by educators. As part of this endeavor, Andrew organized a White House event to bring together EdTech companies, district and state leaders, and other groups. This occasion played a role in kickstarting a nationwide movement known as #GoOpen, which has helped K-12 school districts with things like expanding their use of openly licensed educational materials, getting better discovery and curation tools from companies like Amazon and Microsoft, and getting strategic and sustainability guidance.

Andrew has worked as a teacher and administrator in both the private sector and public education, having served as the Director of Technology for the Grafton Public Schools, the Groton-Dunstable Regional School District, and as an English Literature instructor at several Philadelphia public high schools. In addition, during his time as an instructional technology specialist at Burlington High School, he oversaw one of the first comprehensive 1:1 iPad initiatives in the country. As a result of this effort, Apple recognized Burlington High School as an Apple Distinguished School in 2012. Andrew established and instructed one of the first student-run technology help desks in the country, which went on to serve as a model for other school districts. Students in the "Help Desk" class had the chance to work together with software engineers and take an active role in their education thanks to the course's emphasis on leadership. *The 1:1 Roadmap: Charting the Course for Innovation in Education*, Andrew's debut book, was released in 2014 by Corwin Press.

Andrew earned a Master of Education from Eastern University and a Bachelor of Arts in Communications from the University of Miami in Florida. He resides in North Andover, Massachusetts, with his wife, Caroline, and their chocolate lab, Harper. Andrew is a keen Philadelphia sports enthusiast and he thoroughly enjoyed watching the Phillies 2022 World Series run and the Eagles win the Super Bowl in 2018.

Introduction: From Sharing to Shouting: How Did We Get So Angry?

In 2011, I was part of a team that rolled out one of the first large-scale iPad initiatives in the country. This experience led to my first book titled, *The 1:1 Roadmap*, where I shared this process for implementing a 1:1 program at a public high school in Massachusetts. One of the chapters focused on digital citizenship and teaching students how to use technology and digital platforms for good and to empower their voice. Digital citizenship was still a relatively new term in the lexicon of a classroom, but as students gained greater access to social media, it became very clear it was needed. Students were no longer just engaging in the physical world of school, but there was a burgeoning digital world where they were spending much of their time.

As early as 2011, when I started teaching about digital citizenship, the idea of living in a physical world and an online world was still in its infancy. It was a time when teens and twenty-somethings used Facebook regularly and the Boomers were still trying to select the right input for their DVD player (sorry Boomers). However, in the last decade, much has changed, and access and engagement has increased greatly. Throughout this rapid growth of smart phones and nearly ubiquitous connectivity, much has evolved to lure people in and keep them

"I think I may be developing a Twitter addiction myself!"

DOI: 10.4324/9781003301325-1

there. I often reflect on my first foray into social media back in 2008. I sent my very first tweet on January 26, 2008, and it went a little something like this…

It was such an innocent statement, and I had no idea how this tool worked. But, with my second tweet soon after, you could tell I was getting the hang of it….kind of. I tweeted…

"exploring 2.0 tools for implementation in the upcoming semester!"

As these tools developed and became more accessible to students and educators, the more they became the spaces where we had most of our conversations, connected with family and friends, and shared links and photos. For me, this was a time when I was just starting to see the potential for these tools and how I could teach students to use them in a way that would empower and elevate their voices, rather than diminish them.

As I became more engaged with Twitter and Facebook, I started to make connections through connected educator hashtags and groups that were forming. I engaged in these forums almost daily. I shared links to blog posts and shared lessons I was using in my English classroom. I saw the real power of social media when I was approached by Grace Rubenstein who worked at Edutopia. Edutopia is an educational non-profit founded and funded by the George Lucas Educational Foundation. Grace had heard about a lesson I shared on a blog post where I had students record short videos representing a theme from *Hamlet*. Grace interviewed me over the phone for the piece she was writing, and within a week, the work of my students was being seen and shared by thousands of educators.

Later that same year, after the *Hamlet* post circulated, I was asked by Edutopia if I would be a regular blog contributor for its secondary EdTech market. I gladly agreed and began writing monthly blog posts that focused on using digital tools in the classroom and ways for educators to engage in the sharing spaces of Twitter and Facebook. During the period from when I sent my first tweet until about 2016 is a period I like to refer to as the renaissance period of social media. It wasn't perfect and social media had plenty of dark sides and problems, but for the most part, it was a relatively nice place to engage and learn.

This was also a time when social media was not just broadening my network of people I could share and connect with, but in 2010, landed me an opportunity that I regard as a major career shift. In July 2010, I had unexpectedly lost my job, along with several other colleagues, from a Charter School in West Philadelphia. It was middle of the Summer, and the opportunities for finding a job in education as an English teacher were slim. I decided to write a very vulnerable blog post.

Here is a 2010 excerpt from the blog post:

I have started moving on from my former school and am in the process of seeking out the next path. This journey began on Saturday when I hosted and organized my first unconference at the same school that had just let me go. Not only did I speak positively about the school throughout the entire day, but I promoted their efforts and accomplishments. I have nothing bad to say about my school. They provided so many opportunities for me to grow as an educator and I feel I made a valuable contribution to advancing their curriculum and highlighting ways in which students and teachers can integrate technology more efficiently. I did not want to bring this news with me to edcamp because I wanted edcamp to shine like no other. I put every ounce of my energy into making edcamp the best conference for all in attendance and I am already working towards the next version. edcamp became my only focus and a welcomed distraction from reality.

If you are going to lose your job it helps to have a Personal Learning Network (PLN) behind you to pick you up and get you back on track. I recognize the fact that many people are struggling with joblessness in our country, and this can happen to anyone. The value and support of a PLN will only make this occurrence easier and reinforce that we are never in this business of teaching alone. It also helps to have a conference waiting for you that weekend where most of your PLN will be in attendance. I made a lot of great connections at edcamp and learned a lot throughout the day. I sit back and smile at all the great comments that have been circulating about edcamp and am truly excited for more unconferences throughout the year. Thank you to everyone who made edcamp a shining example of how professional development and personal learning networks can create valuable learning for teachers and in turn benefit all of our students.

Oh, one more thing, if you know of any open positions get in touch with me.

As a result of this blog post and share via Twitter, I received numerous responses from people I knew and people whom I had never met. I shared a very vulnerable experience to a wide audience and received great feedback. I often wonder that if this same scenario happened currently, would I feel comfortable writing the same post, or, for that matter, encouraging a student of mine to embrace vulnerability and share broadly.

So, what happened? And where did we diverge down the wrong path? What I am reminded of in the past three years is the scene in Back to the Future 2, when Marty McFly travels to an alternate time where Biff Tannin runs Hill Valley, and all has gone dark and corrupt. When watching this movie, you realize how precious time is and how easily things can go awry. Part of me feels that many of us, have been so engaged and so distracted by social media that we completely forgot about time and have probably engaged less with those around us. What's more, is that what we are being fed on social media through algorithms created by the companies themselves, were designed to trigger us in a way that hasn't been done before. We all became the mice in the experiment.

And then I read this from *The Washington Post,*

Starting in 2017, Facebook's algorithm gave emoji reactions like "angry" five times the weight as "likes," boosting these posts in its users' feeds. The theory was simple: Posts that prompted lots of reaction emoji tended to keep users more engaged, and keeping users engaged was the key to Facebook's business.

The company's data scientists eventually confirmed that "angry" reaction, along with "wow" and "haha," occurred more frequently on "toxic" content and misinformation.
(Merrill & Oremus, 2021)

I stepped back and reflected for a moment. I was immediately taken back to the 2020 election. I remember posting and engaging on Facebook and Instagram every day leading up to the election. I recall my anger when I would see someone post a message of the other side on one of my posts or when there was news on my feed that made me angry, I would jump into the comments and start verbally swinging. This was not the social media experience I had loved just a few years back; rather, this was a new reality rigged to elicit this type of reaction from me and many others. What Facebook did was play us all and ultimately turn up the heat on what made us angry and, in turn, churned out a profit.

Reading all these leaked papers from Facebook really caused me to pause and examine my relationship with these applications who had done so much for me in the past but were now a source of my anger. What's more, I thought about how to approach this in the context of school. Much of my work in education after launching the 1:1 iPad initiative in Burlington was to support teachers, students, and parents on how to use social media to elevate and empower your voice. But now, the algorithm had turned against us and was leveraging what made us angry to garner profits via clicks. We were no longer controlling the machine, but the machine was manipulating us.

> We were no longer controlling the machine, but the machine was manipulating us.

In the year 2020, lots of negatives seemed to pile on us at once. The pandemic, the election, George Floyd, all tested us to our limits. While we were all quarantined at home, we spent more time on screens and engaged way more with social media and screens in general. So much so, that shows like "Tiger King" became all the rage and fascination. We were stuck at home with little opportunity to engage in person, and while this was all happening, we were sinking further into our tribes behind our screens and taking it out on social media.

As 2020 unfolded, many of the big events of that year created factions in our society when we should have been united. COVID-19 was either a deadly virus, or no big deal designed to steal our freedom away. With George Floyd, you were either outraged at what we all saw or upset that the Black Lives Matter protestors were ruining your city. And all these events culminated to the presidential election which ultimately boiled over into the January 6 attack on the Capitol.

While this was all unfolding, Facebook was generating record engagements with its users and ratcheting up the anger in all our feeds (Merrill & Oremus, 2021). But we didn't realize it. The election eventually ended, but the anger and conspiracies ratcheted up online, Dennis Chauvin was convicted on all three counts of murdering George Floyd, but justice was ultimately not done, and the pandemic continued to fluctuate daily as vaccine conspiracies became the leading cause of those hospitalized. Even as the tumultuous year of 2020 commenced, 2021 was on deck for an angry sequel.

In the last few years, we've entered an "us versus them" culture. This culture plays out daily on social media. Let's take professional sports for example. Each week, numerous college and pro sports game unfold. Many fans watch the game but are more engaged by the memes or clips that result in these games rather than the final score. The final score is finite and doesn't give you much beyond analysis. But what is engaging are the memes, funny clips, a bonehead play being shared instantly on social media while millions of us interpret what that means with complete disregard for the person involved.

Most recently, we've seen this play out at the highest level. This past summer, Simone Biles took a step back from the US gymnastics Olympic team due to strain on her mental health. And she was not alone. Naomi Osaka withdrew from Wimbledon this past summer due to mental health reasons. More and more, we are seeing athletes come forth and speak out about their struggles with mental health. Even professional football, the sport most likened to male toughness, has some of its highest profile players speaking out about their mental health. In many of these cases, the pressures of the games they play are only a fraction of what causes them stress, anxiety, or depression.

The modern athlete must be mentally and physically prepared to compete both on the field and within the realm of social media. The latter of the two is a struggle for many. And not just athletes. Anyone who finds themselves regularly in the spotlight must be mentally prepared to deal with the added pressures that social media adds to the equation. But this task is not just relegated to the rich and famous. Kids in elementary school must understand what these worlds are and how they function. Unfortunately, many students arrive at school with bad social media habits. It becomes the job of the school to repeal these bad habits, and in many cases, the resources just are not there to support. As a result, we see a rise in school counselors needed to support students who are both struggling in school and within digital worlds.

I don't mean to sound pessimistic about where we are and the promise and potential good for social media. But, like any good dystopian novel, this is a warning about what may happen if we don't pause, get offline, assess, and reverse course. We can get there. We can return social media to a better place where voices of the oppressed and often silent can be elevated and make positive change. I think back to the Arab Spring and how social media united people for good and made change that mattered. We don't have to look back that far for the many positive examples of social media use for good.

> We can return social media to a better place where voices of the oppressed and often silent can be elevated and make positive change.

And that's what I hope to convey in the pages ahead. We are still enduring a global pandemic, and many of us don't have the bandwidth to tackle these important issues within a school day and with our kids at home. There is still hope for lowering the temperature on social media and finding ways to elevate and engage with each other in a way that is kind and empathetic. I don't want this book to be a voluminous tome full of lofty words and ideas, but little strategy. I have worked in schools for nearly

20 years. I know what teachers go through day to day and how precious time is in their week. My hope for the readers of this book is to provide them with context for where we are in this space and what we need to do going forward. It's not a silver bullet, but I hope it offers a quick read and actionable solutions that are easy to implement across the content areas and grade levels.

Reference

Merrill, J. B., & Oremus, W. (2021, October 26). "Five points for anger, one for a 'like': How Facebook's formula fostered rage and misinformation." *The Washington Post*. Retrieved December 9, 2022, from https://www.washingtonpost.com/technology/2021/10/26/facebook-angry-emoji-algorithm/

1

Where We're Going, There Are No Rules

Topics Covered in This Chapter:
- ◆ Hiding Behind Masks
- ◆ Digital Ethics and Norms
- ◆ Digital Equity and Inclusion
- ◆ Lens from the Pandemic
- ◆ Navigating Relationships
- ◆ Final Question

Hiding behind Masks

Have you ever experienced road rage? Have you beeped at someone in front of you who doesn't accelerate as soon as the light turns green? Have you actually yelled out of your window at another driver? At some point in our lives, we have all experienced this and have felt the "rage" when someone doesn't follow the rules of the road.

Once the "rage" subsides, did you ever stop and reflect on what provoked that anger? Why you immediately wanted to yell at this person and wish them a bad day? And, all of this when you absolutely know nothing about this person beyond their car

DOI: 10.4324/9781003301325-2

and maybe their face. That's it. In this instance, somebody made a mistake and we just wanted to crush them for it.

I have, as I am sure many of you reading this, been on both sides of this scenario. The side that I find most interesting is the side of the aggressor. In no other situation would I react so angrily in such a quick moment. Have you ever had someone accidentally bump into you while they were not looking and as a result you now have your morning coffee on your shirt? I've seen it happen all the time. And, it's happened to me plenty of times, but, in all of those situations, I have never lashed out at that person for accidentally bumping into me.

What's different in these two scenarios is in one we are, for the most part, protected and masked by the car. In the coffee scenario, we are out there, unmasked and unprotected with people. Human to human. I also realize that both scenarios are not exactly the same since getting your car repaired is a much bigger inconvenience than getting a coffee stain out of a shirt. I get that. But, this also leads me to my point and how we act when we are in our own little bubbles compared to when we are face to face with other humans.

But, the bigger point I am trying to make and I am sure you already figured it out by now, is that we engage in this type of behavior in our daily interactions on social media and through digital tools. And again, I have both witnessed and been engaged in these scenarios. As I mentioned in the Introduction, there have been countless cases of athletes, celebrities, and just regular humans, who have been besieged on social media. It's the digital version of road rage, and it's become a problem across our world. It's led to suicide, mental illness, anxiety, stress, etc. Yet, this kind of behavior happens every day. In some cases, social media companies have removed or banned these individuals who have been the aggressors, but in many cases, it's not enough. Unfortunately, the damage has already been done and it's not easy to come back from.

 ## Pause and Reflect for Students

Have students journal their responses to the questions below. Then, offer time for students to pair up and share, and then share with the larger group.

- Have you ever encountered hurtful comments online?
- How did that make you feel?
- What was your reaction?
- Do you think people act differently online? Why do you think this is true?
- Have you ever acted differently online? Why?

Teachable Moment

Ultimately, what you are trying to do here is understand why someone may be so angry and abusive online, but not be that way in real life. Students should understand that we all have the ability to mask our true self and identity through social media and digital tools such as texting. Additionally, saying you "know someone" online is much different than meeting a new friend or person in real life. Use examples from the previous section to reinforce how social media impacts us all, and there are ways in which we can deal with this type of behavior.

- Log off – The best way to combat abusive rhetoric online is to walk away from it, log off, and tell an adult.
- Delete the app – it could be that it is one application that is causing you stress or anxiety. Take that app off of your phone or tablet.
- Have a real conversation – if someone specifically is targeting you, find them and have an offline conversation about it. Engage with an adult or counselor if this makes you feel more comfortable.

Digital Ethics and Norms

I have been in many face-to-face meetings and Zoom meetings where a group of people come together and the first task is to create norms or conditions for how the meeting and future meetings will carry themselves out. What this process allows for is equity and inclusivity among all members of the group and creates a space where people can speak freely without judgment or ridicule. In essence, it allows for members of the group to bring their best selves to the meeting.

Norm setting sets the stage for equal air-time, allows us to expect the best intentions from our colleagues in the room, and provides a space for everyone to engage in a collegial dialogue in order to solve a problem or advance an agenda item. I have experienced meetings that are not normed from the outset and meetings that are normed. Meetings that are not normed typically are not as productive, you don't hear from everyone and occasionally will walk away from the meeting wondering what just happened or not sure what to act upon after the meeting. While meetings that offer norms and guide rails for the dialogue are seemingly productive, inclusive, and reflective in how they function. The post-meeting feeling is usually an understanding of purpose and action.

In the digital world and on social media, this is not the case. When Snapchat or Instagram was created, it did not gather its users on how they should behave and engage on their respective platforms. Rather, they provide a user agreement that details much of this in very tiny, fine print that all of us blindly click on any given day. There is a great resource to help with this as we find ourselves on any given day, signing up with a digital tool or app and really not knowing what we just signed on to and what information we are giving away and what our rights are on that specific application. Additionally, I have shown this resource to colleagues and my students when discussing and presenting digital health and wellness. It's called Terms of Service Did Not Read (https://tosdr.org). This site assesses the terms of service agreements on many of the most commonly used websites on the Internet and breaks the Terms of Service (TOS) down into layman's terms so that they are digestible and clear.

The setup with digital communications has been frustrating and really unchecked since its infancy. While companies have loosely provided measures for us to conduct ourselves within these online communities, there has not been any guidance beyond the first amendment.

I started using these tools in the late 1990s in the form of Internet Relay Chat or IRC and eventually AOL instant messenger. Both of these tools have since become memes that make my generation feel old, but they started out as the primary way for us to engage with a community by sitting behind a screen. In essence, at the outset of this revolution in communications, our desire to feel connected to people was just getting started. Many of us, including the students we teach daily, did not understand or see the potential for what these tools would bring us. Up until this point, we met in person, wrote and sent letters in the mail, and called people on the phone that was connected to a wall. This all sounds archaic at this point in time, but this is where an entire generation was coming from, and little did I know it would be my generation, those born in the period between the late 1970s and early 1980s that would both take it to great places but also to its darkest.

On the podcast *Offline* with Jon Favreau, Elizabeth Burenig of *The Atlantic* shares insight into how we as humans, with our current set of rules and ethics, are not wired to have everyone talking at once all the time:

> *In the history of humankind, we've never been able to all talk to each other at once before, and I don't think it's something we're actually entirely wired for or sort of wired to like live bands of 20 to 50 and obviously what we're wired for doesn't speak to morally what we ought to do. I think it's great and not morally wrong that we're able to all talk to each other at once and go lots of places and be lots of things. I think that's great, and it's obviously led to many wonderful things but I do think we haven't developed an ethic to deal with it, yet we don't have a moral story about how to be good people with this technology in hand yet we still have ethics that were developed in a time when this kind of Technology was simply not available to us, and so I think that yes the internet technology and our capabilities have developed much faster than our moral story about how to behave in these contexts.*
>
> (Crooked Media, 2021)

Pause and Reflect for Students

Take a moment to reflect on Elizabeth Bruenig's statement and use the questions below to guide your writing:

- Is it a good thing that we have the ability to talk to each other all at once, anytime?
- If you could step back in time before the launch of the Internet, knowing what you know now, what provisions or regulations would you put in place?
- Should there be more regulation around speech on the Internet? Does it fit the definition of the First Amendment to the Constitution? Why or why not?

Teachable Moment

This is a deep topic and students may need some guidance or discussion before launching on their own. This is an opportunity to reflect on mass communication throughout time – the printing press, radio, telephone, television, mobile phone, Internet – and how each impacted society for better or worse.

 Classroom Activity

Divide students into groups and have them take one of the major tools of communication throughout time:

- Printing press
- Radio
- Telephone
- Television
- Mobile phone
- Internet
- Social media
  In their respective groups, have students research each tool and create a campaign for launching each

tool into society. Each campaign should include the following:

- Headline or tagline. Example: "TV: The Window to the Future"
- Points on how it will benefit society
- Campaign ad or poster
- Rules, norms, and regulations for using this tool

Outcomes:

- Students will be able to define the major advancements in communication
- Students will be able to define rules for using these communication tools
- Students will be able to present their campaign for each tool

Digital Equity and Inclusion

At the outset of the pandemic in March of 2020, the world was thrust indoors. Most notably, our students were no longer attending school in person. What was soon realized by many with a blind spot to equity and access is that many of our students were without access or found themselves in challenging scenarios when it came to connecting to "school." What's more, the students who did have access were doing so unfiltered and unguided. What quickly became evident is that the pandemic exposed the gross inequities in our school systems and the level of access to digital health and wellness in their daily classes.

What many assume in education is that all students in 2022 have access to high-speed network access, ubiquitous WiFi, and a device to make all of this possible. However, that is not the case. While we have made great strides toward broadband access for all, many areas of our country are still not wired to support students. According to a report from No Home Left Online by Education Superhighway, 46.9 million households have broadband available in their area but cannot afford to get online (Education Superhighway, 2022). This is two-thirds of America's digital divide, and this is still a pressing issue as more students move ahead with access to technology daily, while so many have access at school but cannot afford to access this basic utility.

What hurts the most in this conversation about equity and access of technology is that, in many regards, technology has helped elevate student voice and agency in many ways. In this sense, technology can be a champion of creating inclusive communities and classrooms. Over the last six years that I have been in schools, I have worked closely with my Director of Diversity Equity and Inclusion (DEI director) to find intersections between the work of the DEI department and technology. And, while this conversation always begins with making sure there is equity of access to tools and resources in our school, the next phase focuses on how we can ensure students are using technology and resources provided to expand the reach of their voice and use technology to champion causes that support all.

At the outset of the pandemic, I had viewed, mostly through social media, an outpouring of support for those directly and indirectly affected by COVID-19. Conversely, I had also witnessed another side of this pandemic that heightened the vast inequities in our country. It was a shame that in the wealthiest country in the world, it took a novel coronavirus to expose and highlight the gross inequities in our American education system as well as the committed passion of those who cared for, taught, and supported our children every day. In America, this should not have been the case. But it was.

Lens from the Pandemic

Below is a post that I wrote on March 18, 2020, just days after the world started to close as the result of the COVID-19 pandemic. I was frustrated, feeling very privileged, and questioning our efforts within social media. It reinforced what the pandemic quickly told us about digital inequities in our schools and how some students would have plenty of access and most would not:

> *As I continue to consume and browse the news, I am reminded of the abundant privilege dump that has taken over many*

social media feeds. The clever parents showing their children doing yoga through their Instagram story, the educator sharing 9000 tips and tricks to support distance learning, the students treating this pandemic as a joke. And listen, I am not perfect, but this is real. For all the positive stories you read and come across, there are so many more that are suffering, filled with anxiety as to what will happen next. This is no hoax, this is not a joke. This is the challenge of our time.

Rather than boast on social media about your team meeting via Zoom, might you consider looking towards areas of need in your educational community. Who has access to food? Who has access to support at home? Who doesn't have access to a computer, a smartphone or broadband? Consider these areas and see where you can support, chip-in, and reach out.

*The Internet can be used for such good, yet it has turned us all into social boasters, ready at an instance to highlight the privilege many of us have. My worry in a world connected so seamlessly and so easily, is the gross amount of misinformation being spread about this pandemic. The hope in times like these is that you have a great leader to guide you through the days and weeks ahead. We do not. As a result, information literacy and understanding what a credible source is, and is **not**, is of utmost importance. We must be mindful to remind ourselves many have support in their families or friends to guide themselves through this time, but many do not.*

During this pandemic, one piece of advice that I have employed and will continue to share is to have empathy. Keep it simple and focused. There are countless resources available, but we do not need to share them all. There are endless memes out there to share, but really think about who that might affect before you share it. And, before you bring us all into the comforts of your home and share how good you have it, cancel that post, and look for ways in which you can support restaurants, schools, and anyone whose livelihood is impacted by this pandemic. Let's all just be good humans and forget about broadcasting it everywhere.

Right now, we are living and writing history each day of this global crisis. Future generations will look back at this time and want to learn from it and understand how to navigate a crisis. How does this generation want to make an impact? How do we want to be remembered? Do we want to be the generation who could use the Internet to make someone laugh? Or do we want to be the generation who demonstrated a human-centered response to a worldwide crisis blending empathy and technology in all the right ways… together?

When we keep moving forward, and leave students behind, we fail entire generations of children. In order to support many of the themes and issues in this book, students must have digital health and wellness embedded across all schools, grade levels, and content arrears in this country. What the pandemic quickly taught us is that not all have access to what many of us now treat as a given in our lives. The way Facebook's algorithms are designed will only further the spread of misinformation and lies and create more conspiracy theories within these forums. All students need a grounding of what truth is and how to evaluate those sources. If we don't create schools where digital equity is ubiquitous, we will continue to spin in circles of distrust and division.

> If we don't create schools where digital equity is ubiquitous, we will continue to spin in circles of distrust and division.

Pause and Reflect for Teachers

The pandemic of 2020 taught us a lot about equity and access to learning resources and opportunities. It also showed us that while we have students in front of us, we can control levels of equity and access by providing resources and ensuring that there are equitable practices in place. What we cannot control is when students leave us at the end of the school day.

- ◆ How can teachers and school leadership collaborate and engage parents so that they can provide similar structure of access and equity at home?

◆ What can we do to support parents at home who may not have all the resources necessary to set up a safe, engaging digital environment for their children?

Resources to support these questions:

◆ https://www.connectsafely.org/
◆ https://www.commonsensemedia.org

Navigating Relationships

When we say we have a connection to someone or are have built a relationship with a person, depending on when we were born, those two phrases mean entirely different things. I am a GenXer and what this typically meant to me is you really got to understand a person, knew a little bit about them and what their passions are, or what makes them tick. When I taught my students, I would spend many of my first few weeks of teaching building relationships with my students in a variety of ways. In all of these instances, technology or social media was not involved.

However, those born after the rise of the iPhone and the access it gives us to social media platforms would most likely say they have a far different definition of what it means to connect with someone or build a relationship. In some cases, those born in the digital age have had a close relationship with a well-lit screen more so than any human in their life. I have seen this unfold as many of my friends and family have kids and always observe how kids engage with screens from the earliest age. In many cases, I often wonder what is best for kids and screens at an early age. The American Academy of Pediatrics (AAP) states that children under two should not be exposed to screens – TVs or devices. While this sounds like sound advice for parenting, according to Anya Kamenetz, this recommendation, "It was based on little evidence. Nine out of ten parents do not follow it" (Crooked Media, 2022).

This data suggests that children at the youngest age are forging a relationship with a screen far before they connect with an adult or peer. Additionally, children are also off in uncharted territory by connecting with people on those screens without context or without norms. This shift in relationship building can and will have an impact on a child's life and may, in some cases, lead to a false sense of what it means to build a relationship with someone outside of a screen.

The challenge here and throughout our digital lives is balance. I am not currently a parent of a child, but working in education I feel that I, and many in this profession, are responsible for guiding children through crucial milestones along their academic journey. In that experience, educators must navigate and build relationships with their students throughout their academic journey. For this, I will rarely give any parent unsolicited advice for how to manage screens or balance the use of technology between home and school. However, when I am asked for advice on this subject, I will often refer back to my teaching days.

I taught in the classroom for twelve years before shifting to an administrative role. And, in that time, I saw classrooms radically transform. It was a time when schools were just starting to get robust wireless connections and email was being widely used by faculty and administration. The iPhone was not an issue in classrooms, and Facebook had just launched beyond a college email address. Later in my teaching career, I worked in a school that was part of a 1:1 technology grant in Pennsylvania. This grant provided every student with a laptop that would reside in charging carts in the classroom. There was minimal training on the tool itself and almost no support or training on how to use these tools to support current pedagogy.

Ultimately, it was a failed experiment that probably turned more faculty members away from the potential of technology in the classroom than engaged them. For students, it was a distraction and used only for word processing and some basic research. And, as a result of this sort of "air drop" technology in the classroom was a now fractured relationship between teacher and student, student and student. The device was now in the way and had more to offer than any human being in that room. A classroom where we once worked on building and fostering relationships now was challenged by a machine.

This trend only worsened as technology became more personal. Educators now face the enormous task of competing with mobile devices that seemingly foster better relationships and have more engaging avenues to pursue at any given moment. Note, that this previous sentence is not to discredit all of the hard work and dedication educators put into teaching, caring for, and supporting students, but more of the reality educators and parents face in trying to navigate relationships with a device present.

It's a challenge we all face on a daily basis and one that has gone mostly unregulated and unmonitored. Couples out at a restaurant both looking down at their phone; people waiting in a line head down on their phones, no matter where we go or what we do, the phone has become the third appendage for all of us.

> So, while there is no silver bullet solution to these behaviors we all engage in daily, there is still an opportunity to strike a balance.

So, while there is no silver bullet solution to these behaviors we all engage in daily, there is still an opportunity to strike a balance. This is where we must step offline in order to thrive online.

Pause and Reflect for Teachers

Think about the way you build relationships with people in your life. What was that process like before mobile technology and social networks? How has that changed with the evolution of social networks?

Pause and Reflect for Students

There are many ways in which we can engage with each other in the year 2022 and beyond. I want you to think about what your definition of a friend is and what it means to build a relationship with someone.

1. What is your definition of a friend?
2. What does it mean to build a relationship with someone?
3. What is your primary way of communicating with your friends?
4. Do you notice your friends act differently when you communicate via a mobile device and when you engage face to face?

Once students complete these four questions, have them pair up and share their answers with each other. As your partner is talking, the listener should answer the following questions:

◆ What did you notice?
◆ What question do you have?
◆ What do you wonder about?
◆ What conclusions can you make?

Optional next phase: Students who are listening can share out to the larger group. Have students who are listening in the larger group interrogate the speaker with the same four questions as above.

Teachable Moment

In that reflection, we are looking for themes and patterns for what students think a friend is and what it means to build a relationship with someone. Really get to the heart of what causes us to act differently when we are engaging via a mobile device or in a social network and why we don't have the same courage or comfort saying the same thing face to face.

Final Question

What are some of the repercussions of acting differently online than when we are in face-to-face contact with that person?

References

Crooked Media (2021, December 19). "Elizabeth Bruenig on forgiving trolls and strangers." https://crooked.com/podcast/elizabeth-bruenig-on-forgiving-trolls-and-strangers/.

Crooked Media (2022, June 5). "Offline with Jon Favreau: How should parents manage kids' screen time? On Apple podcasts." https://podcasts.apple.com/us/podcast/how-should-parentsmanage-kids-screen-time/id1610392666?i=1000565253400

Education SuperHighway (2022, November 1). "No home left off-line: Bridging the broadband accessibility gap." https://www.educationsuperhighway.org/

2

Stepping Off to Step Up

Topics Covered in This Chapter:
- ♦ The Effects of the Pandemic
- ♦ Begin by Stepping Back
- ♦ Developing a New Digital Mindset

The Effects of the Pandemic

When we look back at the year 2020, it will mark a major transition and upheaval in how we functioned as humans. The global pandemic forced all to pivot and adapt to a new way of doing things that stunted us all for a period of time and, for many of us, forced us all on screens. Schools across the nation shut down in-person schooling from March 2020 until the beginning of Fall 2020. Even still, in the Fall of 2020, many students did not return, many faculty members could not return and so schools shifted toward a hybrid way of schooling. For all of us, this meant more time engaged with a screen.

As someone who was on the front lines of designing how a school would work both fully remote and in a hybrid setting, I can confidently share that it is not a natural transition. Even with the expansion of high-speed connectivity and access to 1:1 device environments in many of our schools, what we soon

DOI: 10.4324/9781003301325-3

realized is that the pandemic brought to the surface the still lingering issues of equity among our students. Many students who had access to wireless connectivity and a device in school, in many cases, returned home to limited or no connectivity. What's more, it forced families to live, work, and learn under one roof. While some families had the advantage of ordering desks and accessories to create a remote or hybrid school environment at home, many of our students were huddled in close confines. Additionally, the guide rails that schools' IT departments put in place for filtering and focusing students on using the device for educational purposes were now gone. The pandemic did not just force us all home to work and learn, but it grossly exposed the access and equity divide that still plagues our country.

> *According to the study, published by JAMA Pediatrics, screen time outside of virtual school among teenagers doubled from pre-pandemic estimates of 3.8 hours per day to 7.7 hours.*
>
> *"Kids were essentially putting in a full work day of recreational screen time," said Dr. Michael Rich, director of the Digital Wellness Lab at Boston Children's Hospital and associate professor of pediatrics at Harvard Medical School, who was unaffiliated with the study. "That's a pretty crazy phenomenon when you consider they were also on screens for 5 to 7 hours a day for school."*
>
> (Nagata, 2022)

After assessing these findings, it's clear to see the challenges for educators in a post-pandemic environment. Many of the support systems put in place for our students around screen time and purposeful use of screens were being swiftly pushed by the wayside to ensure some kind of learning could take place while students were home. And while some families most likely created digital at-home policies before the pandemic, there are probably more households that have not. Please don't read that as attacking parents, but rather, having access to resources at school or within your community around these strategies is not a given. Many households don't even have access to the infrastructure where broadband can be accessed at home. And there are even more households where broadband is accessible, but many cannot afford it.

Parents and educators welcomed back students over a year ago to classrooms that did not look and feel the same way they did when they left. As I mentioned before, many students came back to a hybrid environment before fully engaging in a pre-pandemic classroom experience. Some students had to remain home, there was a weekly testing protocol in some cases, and many faculty members needed to be home and teach remotely to a live class full of students. This is not how education was designed to function, and it was a time when both learning loss happened and loss of social skills declined.

One of the biggest issues to arise out of the pandemic that we are starting to see the effects of now is this idea that we were still connected via the Internet and our screens. While this may have seemed like we were connected, this was a misconception that Sherry Turkle has dispelled in her work "Alone Together" and "Reclaiming Conversation." What really happened is that many of us felt alone, scared, and vulnerable in our isolation. This led to many spending more time than usual online and engaging in communities that promoted conspiracies about the pandemic, Dr. Fauci, and vaccines. We saw the rise of QAnon and hate-filled message boards and groups. While many think this was happening on some deep dark web, it was actually happening in plain sight on Facebook.

When we all came back to classrooms and workplaces, we all knew it would be different. What we didn't know is that it would be less kind and angry. Whether it was an email from a colleague or someone at a grocery store, we had gone from singing "we're all in this together" on Zoom to a society divided, angry, and tired. Everything seemed to be awful, all the time. Many were searching for the "why" in all of this, and in many cases, it was a small, but powerful device right in their own hands.

Begin by Stepping Back

This sub-heading sounds impossible when thinking about all the elements educators needed to consider when they helped navigate students to fully remote, to hybrid, to back to school with testing and masking requirements, to somewhat but almost back to normal… but this is how we live now. Also, navigating all that came during this time with the personal ordeals that educators were going through during this time. What educators did during the pandemic is truly heroic and deserves to be commended and acknowledged every chance we get.

But, we must take a step back and think about how we teach and use technology in concert with each other. When I wrote about emerging 1:1 environments back in 2014, I could not foresee how the pandemic would unravel most of the ideas and strategies I was suggesting six years earlier. Many of those strategies were focused on putting the device to use in a purposeful, meaningful way, using classroom technology to elevate and expand student voice, and showcasing diverse opportunities for students to highlight their work. In writing and conceptualizing how this book might help educators and, in some cases, parents, I decided to step back myself and examine these five key areas to reexamine how we, and ultimately, our students, engage with a digital world. What's more, how has the pandemic and the yelling and shouting online impacted us? How do we cut ourselves off from the machine, pause and reflect, and begin to reteach ourselves and our students how to be impactful digital citizens?

Here are five key actions to reexamining how we step back, reflect, define, ask why, and hold ourselves accountable.

1. Self-reflection
2. Substitute nostalgia to step away
3. Define your balance
4. Find your why with digital tools
5. Be accountable

These actions are important for us to really think about why we engage so seamlessly and naturally with a screen. This doesn't mean just simply turning off a screen and saying I am not going to engage with it between the hours of 9 to 5, or that I am going to delete the Instagram app from my phone because that's where I spend most of my time. Those practices, like most fad diets, are not sustainable. Rather, this is an exercise in true self-examination. In the coming chapters, I will dig into these five tenets of screen time accountability that we should first embrace as adults and educators, and that we can share and engage our students in.

When I was writing about this same topic in 2014, I shared a story about a good friend John Spencer who abstained from Facebook for 40 days. He called it the living Facebook project and he would write about his daily interactions with people and things. He shared how instead of pinging someone via Facebook to see if they wanted to play Words with Friends, he would walk up to a stranger at a Starbucks and ask them if they wanted to play scrabble. I shared this with my students and, at the time, asked them to abstain from Facebook for one week. NOTE: *this is back when teenagers actually used Facebook.*

During this abstinence, my students would write about their experiences without Facebook and share in class. The conversations focused around responses like, "I never realized how much time I waste." or "I have a better sense of what is going on around me." or "I feel more connected outside of social media than I did engage in it." At the time, I was surprised by how much my students responded. Despite this effort, it was only a temporary fix. It was not sustainable.

 ## Pause and Reflect for Students

Have you ever truly disconnected from social media? What was the experience like in the moment? How did it make you feel? Were you eager to get back? Briefly journal how your offline experiences have been. If you have not had any, write about the times you are away from your phone or social media accounts. How did these moments make you feel? What did you do in place of it?

Teachable Moment

This is a great opportunity to really get students to see how their conversations and relationships happen online and offline.

Many of our students don't know how to navigate a day let alone a few hours without a connected device. This is also a good opportunity to engage parents in this topic. As teachers, we only see students for a brief period of time throughout the day, but parents typically begin and end the day with their kids. During these times at home are the most prevalent times when students are engaged on their phones.

Developing a New Digital Mindset

For many of us of a certain age 40–50ish, we can remember a time when boredom was a thing and creativity was at an all-time high. When we break down the ease of access that a mobile phone brings us, coupled with applications designed to engage, it's no surprise we spend countless hours consuming information via a small, pocket-sized screen. However, this was not always the case. Growing up in the 1980s was peak excitement and creativity when it came to kids and entertainment. Obviously, as a child of the 1980s, I am biased toward this decade, but when I reflect upon it, I feel it was peak creativity for young kids. We had to be. We didn't have all of these options and avenues for communication in our pocket, all the time. The phone was connected to the wall and a copper wire. The Television only had about 30 channels. The radio needed to be tuned, and music was still a physical thing we could hold in our hands. Making mix tapes was an event that you planned with your friends and cousins. If you were lucky, you had a VCR, a camcorder, and a Nintendo Entertainment System. If you were very lucky, like my friend James, you had the Nintendo with Rob the Robot (My wife eventually got me this system for my 40th birthday). People drove their cars without looking down, kids played outside as long as allowed, and people read physical newspapers and magazines. Conversation was our opportunity to speak out. Reflecting back on this time in the year 2022, I realize that everything I mentioned is accessible through one singular device that fits in my pocket.

I am not making an attempt to be nostalgic, but when I consider my childhood, our mindset was always set to creative ways to engage and have fun – whether that be making a mix tape, listening to your favorite radio host with a blank tape in the boom box so you could record your favorite song, or riding bikes around town in the summer until the sun went down. Kids of this generation had to create, imagine, and design on the fly. We didn't have everything at our disposal, all the time.

When I was setting out to sketch out this section in this chapter, I wanted to think about the limitations we had on our technology when I was growing up and how that pushed our thinking and creativity. I also wanted to build a bridge to today's generation and think about ways in which they will create and design in their future, but with the difference of their ability to consume more than they create or ideate.

I recall an experience I had with my five-year-old nephew, Charlie. Charlie got into video games pretty quickly when he came to visit our house last summer. The PlayStation 5 was fairly new, and he was amazed at the graphics, the 3D worlds designed in the gameplay and the engaging music and controller. I mean, I was blown away by it too. We came a long way from those 8 bit days of thick pixelation. Later that day, I decided to switch out the PlayStation and hook up my original Nintendo Entertainment System. I grabbed the Super Mario Brothers game, blew on the inside, and then wiggled it into place. That act alone, took me back to so many good days, with friends, trying to beat the next level in our pursuit of being the first kid on the block to beat the game and win the day. I gave Charlie the controller that was not wireless and explained what the handful of buttons did. As he started playing, the Mario character jumped up and hit a box that contained a mushroom. The mushroom started moving and eventually went to the left of the screen. Charlie tried to quickly move Mario in that direction, but it was too late. He looked up at me with a stunned face and said, "Why can't I go back and get the mushroom?" I didn't have an answer. No one ever asked me that.

What I immediately realized from this exchange was that he was developing his own creative mindset and interrogating what is, so that he, or maybe someone in his generation, will solve this problem and make it better. The same way we did when we were kids. We interrogated the way things were and tried to design and figure out how things could be better in order to make attempts at solving problems. When we went to the music store and bought a tape or a CD, we got all the songs by that artist. But, in many cases, we just wanted the popular single. So, we solved this by using the tools and technology we had to make mix tapes.

However, my worry with today's generation is that when I was growing up, we could focus on imaging or visioning the future. When I read the book *The Road Ahead* by Bill Gates, I was blown away when he described that all the technology we have today will be accessed in a piece of hardware the size of a wallet. From that moment on, I thought about what that might be like and how we could use these emerging technologies someday. Little did I realize that much of the good these tools would provide society, that the negative impact of them would greatly outweigh the positive. The problem with having all the information all at once, all the time, and access to groups of friends and people we don't know 24/7 is that it doesn't give us time to process and imagine. Instead, we are trapped in these loops we cannot escape that prevent us from moving on from the past, and that create a level of anxiety in us all that make it so we can hardly think about a positive future.

As users and consumers in a digital world, it's easy to lose the sense of creativity and problem solving when everything seems to be done for us and, in some cases, easy. I even thought about this concept when I was thinking of writing this book. Does anyone want to read a book anymore? Would I be more successful if I sent a bunch of tweets on this subject and started a podcast? Maybe. But, probably not considering Twitter has become an unchecked wasteland of misinformation, hate, and unhinged conspiracy theories by "verified" users who paid $8. But, I digress.

My point in this chapter and what I hope to get across to educators and students is that we must leverage the technology and digital tools we have available to us, to solve problems and push our current technologies further by providing opportunities and access for all of our students. What I worry about is that many of our students and adults (Boomers too) get thrown into these digital worlds and simply hang out there and consume. They scroll, they occasionally shout or share, but are just spinning in circles, living a life in the past.

I know this is true because I have seen it happen to me on numerous occasions. And what's easy about these digital worlds is that they are ripe for all of us to pile on. We pile on so much that we forget what we were even arguing or debating. As I mentioned earlier in this book, I needed to step back from Facebook after the 2020 election. The algorithm was keeping me engaged and angry by what I saw each day on my news feed. I took it personally and wanted to battle everyone and pile on every chance I got. I soon found myself just reading comments on other's posts and jumping in and digitally swinging and piling on in those forums. And for what? Because I thought maybe I would change someone's vote? That I would get a comment of the year trophy? When I stepped back, paused, and reflected on this and the entire election cycle, what I soon realized was that it was all a giant waste of time. It was out of my control and the machine was designed to keep me angry and engaged on the platform. Ultimately, I accomplished nothing, had to apologize to people, and looked foolish.

If we don't make concerted efforts to change and evolve our digital mindsets, then we are doomed to live in these feedback loops of the past that go nowhere and accomplish nothing for us. The only winner in these spaces are the owners, investors, and advertisers of social networks. We are simply doing all the heavy lifting while programmers and coders sit back and watch their intentionally designed algorithm take hold.

In the following chapters, we will begin our journey on designing a new digital mindset. Ultimately, this transition begins with us as adults and provides us ideas and strategies to be good digital role models for our students. We don't want to just take technology away or restrict access. Access is power, but we must provide guide rails and coordinates so

> Access is power, but we must provide guide rails and coordinates so that our students can navigate and traverse a congested, volatile digital landscape.

that our students can navigate and traverse a congested, volatile digital landscape.

 ## Pause and Reflect for Students

The use of digital tools and almost ubiquitous network infrastructure has ensconced us in rapid fire information and access everything and everyone we need at any given moment of our day. Think about how you use these tools on a daily basis and why you use these tools. Is your primary use entertainment, communication, learning? Do you think this constant access has influenced the way you think? And do you think it has influenced how you engage with friends and family?

Teachable Moment

As we enter the next few chapters, this is the moment where you want students to begin thinking about their daily interaction with digital tools. What many students of this generation may miss is how much these tools influence us and the affect they have on our thinking. According to LM Sacasas, "The Internet has trapped us all in a doom loop constantly circling us in the past" (Atlantic Media Company, 2022). Check in with students on how they react to these ideas and if they feel like they are trapped in a past loop that just keeps circling them back to information and content that is no longer current.

Think about ways in which students can step back and offline from digital worlds and what would be a good plan to for them to step back and offline? These questions will all be addressed in the coming chapters, but begin to plant the seeds and see if students have ever thought about these concepts. The reality of creating a new digital mindset that begins with stepping back and offline is to first realize, as adults, that most of our students were thrust into these worlds without any understanding of their influence and potential. Anyone born after 2007 immediately became part of the iPhone generation. These kids are currently 15–16 years old now and are fully impressed in their high school years.

References

Atlantic Media Company. (2022, June 13). "How the internet became a doom loop." *The Atlantic.* Retrieved December 9, 2022, from https://newsletters.theatlantic.com/galaxy-brain/629ec16551 acba002091af11/internet-social-media-reactionary-doom-loop/

Nagata, J. M. (2022, January 1). "Screen time use among us adolescents during the COVID-19 pandemic." *JAMA Pediatrics.* Retrieved December 9, 2022, from https://jamanetwork.com/journals/ jamapediatrics/fullarticle/2785686

3

Engage in Self-reflection

Topics Covered in This Chapter:
- ♦ It Begins with Adults
- ♦ Smartphone Audit
- ♦ Create Goals

It Begins with Adults

In the last five years or so, there has been a debate on the best time for children to get a smartphone or old-school cellphone. I have presented on digital health and wellness many times, and it is the number one question I receive from parents, family members, and friends who all are in pursuit of this golden answer. However, I don't think there is much debate here at all. Before we can answer that question as responsible adults, we need to do our own self-reflection on how we, as responsible adults in the room, use our cellphone.

Those of us of a certain age can remember a time when we used to do almost everything in plain view of our parents. We did our homework at the table, talked on the phone connected to a wall, and watched television or played video games in a shared space in the house. Writing this makes me sound old, but that was the reality when I grew up in the 1980s and early 1990s. The

DOI: 10.4324/9781003301325-4

sense of privacy in one's home was none. Very rarely could my brother or I go into our rooms, shut the door, and engage in any activity beyond sleeping. I am surprised we even had doors on our rooms, come to think of it.

When I was growing up, the debate was focused on when was the right time for us to have a television in our rooms or a telephone. But, I mention all of this for a reason. As technology evolved and I grew up, things became more and more private from our parents. We went from talking on the phone in our kitchen to having a phone in our room to having a computer in our house to having a computer with Internet access to a mobile phone in our pocket to an iPhone with social applications to a device that has social applications designed to enhance one's ultimate privacy. It's a long journey, but with every step of that journey, I gained more and more privacy from anyone around me. Eventually, the device and all that came with it became the center of my universe.

Throughout my upbringing, one piece of developmental psychology that impacted most of what I did from the time I was a toddler through my adolescent years was the influence of my parents and grandparents. I watched and modeled every move they made. I watched how my Dad watched TV and laughed loudly every Thursday night when watching *Cheers*. I paid close attention to how my Mom used the phone in the house and made every move necessary to avoid the incoming cord that would almost always get tangled. This is how most of us learn during our formative years, and this is why I bring this up as the first place for adults to examine how they use a smartphone daily before deciding whether or not to provide their children with their own phones.

The same formula can be used by educators in the classroom. How frequently are you using your phone throughout the day? How often are you doing this within sight of your students? In most cases, as students grow and advance in grades, they develop habits that are influenced by many factors. As educators, we spend countless hours in front of students. Every second of those moments together, students pick up on things we do and say. They are also bringing with them their habits, good or bad, that they acquired at home. Almost always, students come to the classroom with passive digital skills. That is, they are all excellent consumers of whatever happens to be on the screen. But, they are not skilled in the active use of technology to create, design, and develop efficiencies in their day.

Smartphone Audit

Ultimately, this is where we, as adults, need to conduct a smart-phone audit on how we use this tool each day. To begin, we must start by making a three-column chart.

Once you have conducted this audit, you need to examine your notifications and any devices these may hit. This includes, but is not limited to, your smartwatch and any smart devices that present a distraction. For example, alerts on your desktop when you're working alerting you to an arbitrary email. My suggestion to start, turn off notifications. Honestly, we don't need them. The more I look at my phone, watch, or desktop at the barrage of notifications that come up at any given moment is so unnecessary, and both distract me and cause me to lose focus on what I am doing.

To write this book and get it done within my timeline, I needed to cut the notifications and really organize my phone. In the chart above, I kept the "Need to use" column of applications on my phone and limited my use of notifications. I turned off email notifications, for example, and kept on text notifications. For emails, I created check-in points for my emails. I would add these times to my calendar in 10-minute increments. This was also preceded by some messaging that I did not consider an

Need to use (work and personal)	Like to use (social media)	An open bag of candy (games, etc.)
Gmail	Instagram	Two dots
Slack	Snapchat	CandyCrush
Google maps	TikTok	
Google drive		
Banking apps		

email an emergency. If you need me immediately, please call. And that was it.

The apps in the middle column you can delete from your phone entirely or just move off the home screen. I have an iPhone, so I moved those apps into my app library, away from my home screen, and turned off the notifications. This one can be a struggle and also reinforces the addictive nature of scrolling endlessly, looking for who knows what. It's the equivalent of driving around aimlessly until you see someone pulled over or see a crash. There's no purpose to it other than to see what everyone else is doing.

I have cut the middle column apps cold turkey before. I simply deleted the apps from my phone. It was very difficult, but when I returned, I realized I had not missed much. I could keep pace with world events and happenings simply by reading a newspaper or watching the nightly news. For friends and family, I found I started to have richer conversations and more to say to them when I deleted these apps. I had questions about what they were doing, did they go on any trips, and how was the new job, for example. In many cases, accessing someone's life through a very accessible device removes a lot of conversation and questions from our lives. It doesn't allow us to live in the moment as we are always trying to capture it and share it with others, nor does it allow us to engage meaningfully when we connect with someone in real life.

Much of what I just wrote became evident to me roughly ten years ago when I attended a Paul McCartney concert at Fenway Park. As soon as Sir Paul took the stage, everyone's screens rose in unison and took photos or videos of the famed Beatle. I myself was doing the same thing. But I wondered, who am I attending this concert for, me or them? Them being the masses, friends, and family eagerly waiting by their phones at home wanting to experience some aspect of this concert. This was no way to experience a once-in-a-lifetime concert; standing on the field of one of the most storied ballparks in America, watching one of the most famous Beatles perform music, and I was putting a screen in front of my face and creating a filter of my reality at that moment. This was no way to experience this show.

Create Goals

Once you have done an audit of your own phone, you'll want to try it out for a week or so. See how it feels and develop new habits. Don't just cut everything all at once because it's very easy to get frustrated and want to return to how it was. So, after your week of trying out your post-audit phone, reflect on how it felt and begin to jot down some goals and action items. Goals should be things you hope to accomplish with your new phone dynamic. For example, see the chart below on goals I have set for myself.

With each of these goals, I am taking steps to put my phone audit to work and progress up toward a long-range goal of being more present with events, nature, and daily life. To measure these goals, I highly recommend getting yourself a journal and tracking your days and how you engage, how many books you read, and some reflections on the conversations you had. Also, make sure you log in the moments where it didn't go so well. Give yourself a rating each day. For example, I scored myself a two today because I started doom scrolling on Twitter and started getting into arguments with complete strangers who I didn't even know. This method allows you and your students to track and measure your success.

You may also want to have a partner you do this with and have check-ins over the phone or in person to see how you both are progressing and areas where you are struggling. Having an accountability partner is a great way to stay on track for your goals and feel like you are on the road to accomplishing your goals.

This chapter is the first step toward understanding your habits, setting your goals, and holding yourself accountable. Everything in this chapter is not only designed for adults to

Short-term goal	I want to read more books
Mid-range goal	I want to have more engaging conversations with friends and family who I typically find out on social media
Long-range goal	I want to be more present in events, nature, and daily life

begin their reflective journey toward being more engaged out-side of a smart device but can also be introduced to students as early as elementary school.

For most of us, technological devices have been introduced into our lives rapidly. They show up and change how we live our lives, but at no time, do we fully understand the long-term outcomes, nor do we follow a set of norms to keep us grounded and ensure we are not falling down the path toward addiction. These spaces where we spend so much of our time and energy go relatively unchecked. No one is out there policing comments or providing real-time checks and balances on those who are spreading vitriol, nor is there anyone checking in on how we are doing as we view these comments or posts that may impact or trigger us. How we think and act since the advent of the smart-phone and all the applications that come with us has changed dramatically. It has changed the way we teach, the way we parent, and the way we engage with society at large.

> It has changed the way we teach, the way we parent, and the way we engage with society at large.

When I engage with social media, all I see are people sharing their good moments and happy times. While this is great and all, it assumes that we, as friends or consumers of this content, feel happy and thrilled for them. But, what really happens is it makes us sad. So many women can't bear children or think of those who have lost loved ones and have to endure the stream of social posts on Mother's Day or Father's Day. We must make an effort to step back and step off-line in order to begin designing and living a new digital mindset, and really make an effort to audit our actions and engagements with these tools.

 Pause and Reflect for Teachers

When you conducted your smartphone audit, how did it make you feel? What did you do when you were not scrolling or engaging on applications? Did you feel disconnected or more connected to your family and friends?

Teachable Moment

This chapter is about stepping back and really examining our daily habits that center around the smartphone. I spend so much of my day on my phone, but when I do put it away, I feel connected and engaged more than when I am on it. I also spend a great deal of my time while I am traveling or commuting to work observing the people around me on their devices. What I notice more than ever before is people with their heads down in their phones. I see this in restaurants, at family gatherings, while driving, while walking, and so many more. This is also present inside and outside of schools. Educators make a big impression on students at the youngest age. However, working in a school for my entire career, I also realize that the smartphone can be used as a teaching tool and is a crucial tool in an emergency.

 Activity for Teachers

Think about ways in which you and your colleagues use a smartphone that promotes positive, purposeful use of the technology. List these out and work in groups to discuss. Then, think about your technology Acceptable Use Policy that all students and faculty sign off on each year. And answer the following questions:

- ◆ Is it clear what we are asking of students?
- ◆ Do I teach these concepts within my classroom? If so, please share.
- ◆ How can I teach these concepts within my classroom.

Outcome

In order to be able to implement a policy, you, yourself have to be able to live and adhere to that policy. The goal of this exercise is to really examine your technology use within the school. Also, to examine your governing document around technology use in the school. What you want to come out of this activity is a dialogue around how technology is being governed in the school and if there are ways you can ensure these topics are taught to students. You and your colleagues should be able to build out a repository of lessons that you can all share and adapt within your classroom.

4

Leverage Nostalgia

Topics Covered in This Chapter:
- ♦ Look to the 1980s and 1990s
- ♦ Reclaim Conversation
- ♦ Make Meaningful Connections

During the pandemic, one of the things we lost was time together. The ability to feel and connect with someone on a personal level within the same space. However, despite the pandemic and all the isolation it brought with it, this redesign of human interaction had already started to change. Many wondered what the pandemic would be like if it happened in the 1980s or 1990s? How would we have connected or even held school during that time. It crossed my mind as I was writing this book and especially this chapter. And, the short answer is, we would have been fine.

The reality of the digital age is that while the perception of us gaining so many new advances is true, we are just engaged with new tools and doing the same things as previous generations. There's an image floating online showing business men in the old days on a train reading newspapers and not looking at each other, and it says "All This Technology Is Making Us Antisocial" (https:// medium.com/alt-ledes/stop-sharing-this-photo-of-antisocial-newspaper-readers-533200ffb40f). The image frustrates me and

DOI: 10.4324/9781003301325-5

provides a skewed perception of how technology has changed us as a society. While out of context, this image represents a time when humans were engaged with the print medium but assumes they were not engaged with each other or anything around them.

Technology infrastructure through the Internet, the advent of the mobile phone, and the rise of social media applications have completely changed the way we think, the way we engage, and the way we consume information. In each of these instances, we have regressed and, according to Max Fisher, in his new book *The Chaos Machine*, become angrier and more divided. And, while the image of the men reading newspapers on a train may seem like we were always a disengaged, consumer-driven people, what it doesn't layer on is that the content they were reading did not utilize a machine learning algorithm designed to push newspaper articles in your face that made you angry. And, this is exactly what Facebook has been doing since it replaced "The Wall" with the "Newsfeed."

Look to the 1980s and 1990s

So, how are we supposed to, as educators or parents of children, teach against a mood-altering drug that 80% of the population take at least 12 times a day? That's a question that struck me while listening to the "Offline" podcast with Jon Favreau. Throughout the writing of this book, I have been engaged with this podcast and it has really pushed my thinking in many ways. The podcast was just coming online as I was beginning this book and throughout my time listening to it, I thought about the period in which I grew up.

Many of us born at the outset of the 1980s entered a world where much of the Silicon Valley elite were still tinkering in garages and, by many, considered nerds. Most of the technology and innovations created in Silicon Valley would not touch my hands for another 20 years. And, while some of my first engagements with a screen were a passive experience on the television, much like the newspaper photo referenced earlier, it was a one-way engagement. I couldn't touch and engage with the TV screen, I couldn't speak to or Tweet at the characters on the screen, and while TV producers tried their hardest to keep us on their channel, I could leave at any time and not feel the anxiousness of needing to go back. While screen time in the 1980s and 1990s was more of a passive and patient experience, it did change the way I think and learned as a child. But, it did not create an addiction that caused me anxiety and stress.

In March of 2020 when the world started to shut down as a result of the pandemic, I was drawn to the way people were keeping themselves engaged and away from screens. You had people making bread, completing puzzles, and playing scrabble by the fireside. It was a fascinating period and one we can learn a lot from. During this time, most of us, including our children, were engaging on a screen in every facet of their lives. School, work, and social engagement and entertainment all became screen-based endeavors. It was rewarding to hear about people engaged in other types of ways outside of obsessively "doom-scrolling" through social media and away from shouting on Twitter about the validity of Dr. Fauci. When students eventually returned to their classrooms, things were different, and the amount of screen time and bad habits had increased in the lives of children significantly.

And while we were spending our days on the screen at work and then after work all within the confines of our home, we were all getting burned out by the screens. Many of my colleagues experienced Zoom fatigue in which they spent almost their entire day meeting within Zoom's small rectangle box among a gallery of them. Soon, we became very tired of the phrase "You're on mute." As someone who has worked their entire career to implement new and emerging technologies into classrooms, this was not the recommended approach to bringing new users to the technologies. In fact, my biggest worry was that screen fatigue would have a negative effect on adults as they returned to the classroom or the office and ultimately lead to less teaching about how to purposefully use technology tools.

While the jury is still out on how the pandemic changed us as a society and studies and books (like this one) are just now being written on the subject, it's not that hard to see how most of us just picked right up where we left off. In education, this was also the same.

In a post-pandemic school environment, which many of us find ourselves as I type this, it's not as easy to say that we all need screen-time detox. It's not that easy. And, for educators, it is even more complicated as many of our students returned to classrooms with these bad habits around screen time. This is what I encouraged in this five-point plan (self-reflection, nostalgia, balance, your why, be accountable) for balancing screen and non-screen time and ensuring we as adults go through it in order to model well for our students.

 ## Pause and Reflect for Teachers

Think about your pandemic experience. What were some of the biggest changes at the outset of the quarantine in March 2020? How much a part of your day was technology? Did you experience screen fatigue?

After you answer those questions, think about ways in which you stepped away from the screen and technology. What analog activities did you start doing? Do you still do them? What new things did you learn?

When you have completed the two sets of questions, group up with some colleagues and share your experiences. Find common themes and think about ways in which you can leverage your collective experiences to bring some of these concepts into the classroom?

Outcome

While we don't quite realize it yet, we learned a lot about ourselves during the pandemic. What's more is we also learned a lot about our families and friends. We were forced to slow down and remain isolated from each other. In the moment, we all persevered because as humans we are resilient strong beings who can thrive in the face of adversity. For many, this was also a good time to examine ourselves and our practices. As I mentioned earlier, many of us found alternatives to technology. And, while we still want to make sure we teach our students how to use technology purposefully, we also want them to realize the alternatives.

Reclaim Conversation

I want to begin this sub-heading by recognizing the title of it is also an amazing book by the same name from Shelly Turkle. This book was released in 2016 which seems to be a benchmark point when we look at when we started becoming very angry and divided in our country. Not because of any political figure, but rather this was the beginning of the divide that was elevated by financially driven practices by social media companies like Facebook.

In the opening chapters, I talked about how and why I decided to leave Facebook. During 2020, I found myself constantly checking Twitter and Facebook for what was happening with the pandemic, Black Lives Matter protests, and the Presidential election. I also noticed my actions both on the platform and outside of it. In short, I felt angry all the time. So, after the election, I decided to leave. I left my Facebook account active, but aside from checking in occasionally, I was not posting anything nor engaging in comments. It's now been two years like this, and I can honestly say I feel better and engage more effectively with the world around me and my family and friends. I don't feel angry anymore, because I have read and researched how companies like Facebook designed their algorithms to keep us all actively engaged on their platform and actively angry on their platform.

While I was in the Facebook wilderness, I found myself reflecting a lot on my time on the platform and my time away. Most importantly, I thought about how educators would prepare students for a world in which machines are playing games with our moods and ultimately causing anger, stress, and anxiety in our children. In short, there is no silver bullet here, but unlike when I was teaching students to use social media and the Internet to elevate their voice and their talents, I now found myself talking to parents and students to maybe hold off on getting their child signed up for a Twitter account, or maybe start with a flip phone before rushing them into a world where everyone is shouting, no one is listening, and no one is being kind.

When I was in the classroom teaching, I would teach students how to have a conversation online before allowing them to actually engage in a conversation online. For most of my students, they were already engaging in online discussions through Facebook, Snapchat, Twitter, and Instagram to name a few. So here is what we did:

1. I broke up the room into four or five pods.
2. On each pod, I placed a large piece of easel paper and some markers.
3. In the center of each easel paper, I drew a large circle with a topic. (Usually, this is something that we read or about a subject we were discussing but can really work for any subject matter.)
4. Students were grouped around each pod. Their rules were:
   a) No talking.
   b) You have a conversation by drawing a line from the center circle and writing your response or your comment in that circle. Their peers could choose to start their own thread or contribute to an existing one.
   c) What they wrote in the thread had to continue the conversation thread in an engaging way. For example: You wouldn't write "Nope" when continuing a thread.
   d) Every five minutes the pods would rotate and engage in a new conversation at their next pod.
5. When we ended this activity and everyone made it through each pod, we would first have a discussion reflecting and interrogating this process of communication.
6. At the end of this conversation, we would then begin to draft our norms for online communication threads and how we would work within our Learning Management System or LMS.

There are a lot of pros to an activity like this and involves nostalgic, non-screen engagement that had the students focus on the conversation and the people around them rather than just shouting what they thought out into an unmoderated or normed environment. The students had parameters and couldn't speak to each other verbally. So, this activity, in many cases, emulated an online discussion where more often than not, we find ourselves as Sherry Turkle coined, Alone Together. Additionally, this exercise reinforces the necessity for our students to learn how to engage offline, before they are thrown out into the depths of the Internet and experience all that comes with it for better or for worse.

The activity I just shared and all that comes with it should be the way in which we not only engage with our students as teachers and parents but also drop the notion that just because someone is born in a certain age, that they are assumed to be digital natives. This idea had been pushed in many forums over the last ten years. And, while students probably have less fear about engaging with technology hardware and digital applications than some adults, it does not make them an expert on how to use these tools effectively. In many cases, students are simply consuming content and not creating, designing, and producing. Even with the advent of Instagram Reels and Tik Tok, most of the content I consume on there is by a select few of "influencers" and not your regular kid. But, this is yet another opportunity for educators to bring in the design frameworks of these tools and leverage their design to teach students how to responsibly use these tools. Here is an example.

 ## Classroom Activity: Tik Toking Our Online Norms

Thinking about the activity I just shared regarding online conversations, what I would typically do next is have students build out and own their online discussion norms. And, while this is just for our Learning Management System and Google Docs discussion, I make sure to encourage them to follow these norms when they are out in the wild world of social media.

1. Students can pair up in groups.
2. Task: create an in-person Tik Tok to demonstrate your norm for online discussions.
   a) Students should story board their Tik Tok.
   b) Select a song and dance moves of their choice.
   c) Pick a specific hashtag for their norm and explain why it should be trending.
3. Students can use the "clips" app from Apple and shoot it on a classroom iPad.

Make Meaningful Connections

Learning digital citizenship is a fairly new category in the student course list. In the past, students were taught to be civil and work toward being impactful citizens in their society. The principle of citizenship is entwined in many school mission statements as well. In the past, bullying, teasing, and fighting were seen as "childlike" behaviors and addressed as necessary. Students were told at an early age to play nicely together, to share, and not to call each other names. While these events still happened, they did not have the reach and appeal of today.

With the launch of data networks, almost ubiquitous WiFi, and the smartphone, adults and students alike now share a platform for consuming and authoring information as our society has never seen. Today's networked world gives everyone a voice, a digital space, and a bullhorn to be heard. While this freedom of expression is nothing new to our society, the medium is taking us into uncharted territory. So, how do we integrate standards and skillsets that prepare our K-12 students for an interconnected, digital world that can often be incendiary and hurtful? The unfortunate answer is that we are already too late in some regard. Applications and the pace of technology have outpaced our ability, as parents and teachers, to keep up with what our students can access.

However, this is not to say that we can't teach our students proper digital health and wellness skills. One of the key issues is teaching kids offline before they jump into an online world. They need to know the harsh realities of a networked world, discern between their real offline personality and tailored online personality, and understand that both personalities should be the same. They still need to know how to play nicely together, share, not tease or say hurtful things – and they need to transfer these offline skills to a digital space as well. In short, students must understand that there should be no difference between how they act online and how they act offline.

Elementary Skillsets

Here are some quick ideas for integrating these basic skillsets into the elementary grades:

♦ Have students write a letter to each other and then to someone beyond the school. This reinforces the transferable skill of writing offline to writing online. It's a great way of introducing email and understanding that the digital world also speaks English and uses the conventions and formatting of proper grammar.

♦ Have students create something on a large easel paper (a drawing, poem, short sentence, etc.). Once completed, ask them to walk around the room as if they were in a museum and make comments on each creation. This is a great way of having students comment in public and provide authentic feedback that is constructive and kind.

♦ Digital spaces should not be painted as dark, negative environments. Students should understand how great opportunities might come their way when they construct and maintain a positive digital presence. Students entering middle school should be able to:
  • Generate safe usernames.
  • Discuss the difference between personal and private information.

- Explain why there are logins and passwords for some hardware, software, and websites.
- Describe why stealing information and other people's creations is the same as stealing tangible items.
- Use technology to explore personal interests.
- Demonstrate to others how to use technology tools in ways that assist rather than prevent learning.

This list is not complete, but it offers a good foundation of what elementary-level students should be expected to know as they move up to middle school. As students climb through the grade levels, these skills increase. Once in middle school, students should begin to understand:

- How to start gathering research both online and offline.
- How to discern between credible sources and misinformation.
- How to interact within digital spaces (i.e. a Google Docs, social media apps, or a Learning Management System).
- How to properly find and cite digital media (creative commons, Google Docs, research tools).
- How to discern between positive and negative use of digital spaces and the possible consequences of inappropriate behavior.

By the time students get to secondary grade levels, they should be expected to exhibit positive and consistent digital citizenship skills. I've always liked the idea that students graduating from middle school should have to pass a digital citizenship "driver's ed" course. This test would demonstrate an understanding of the basic standards of what it means to be a digital citizen. At schools that employ 1:1 programs, this would be a good way of obtaining the keys to your device. Below is an example of a project that I did with ninth grade students. I have included the lesson plan and the rubric I used to assess student work.

Classroom Activity: Getting Your Digital Citizenship Driver's License

Digital Health and Wellness Project

Today, we are about to embark on another exciting project. Once again, our class must come together as a team and create a comprehensive guide for understanding digital citizenship and knowing how to take care of your digital identity.

Objective:

Promote awareness on maintaining your digital identity and understanding your web privacy.

Expectations:

- ♦ Work collaboratively.
- ♦ Develop, design, and populate a digital space that is interactive and engaging for our information and media.
- ♦ Research topics dealing with digital citizenship and digital privacy.
- ♦ Create various forms of media to promote digital citizenship awareness among students and adults.
- ♦ Engage and respond daily.

Project Teams:

Research and Development

This team will be responsible for gathering information for the project. They will find resources for social media posts, create surveys for data collection, and put together the content for the production team. This team will have to work in conjunction with the production team and the social media teams. The R&D team will not only gather resources for others to use and cite in their work, but they will have to create thorough surveys to collect data.

Social Media Team

This team will be responsible for showcasing our content. They design and create posts that cover one of the above topics. Create media outlets for our site through Twitter, Instagram, Facebook, etc. and build a network of followers online to discuss digital citizenship talks. This could be in the form of Google Meet or Zoom discussion on digital health and wellness subjects. This team is constantly moving and shaking; trying to stay ahead of the curve and keep the information current and fresh.

Production

This team will work in conjunction with the research and development team to take their research and turn it into media. They will be in charge of creating storyboards, creating scripts, filming videos, conducting interviews, and editing final products. In short, all of the media that is created will be done by this team. This team will not all be working on one video but several productions within the team. It is imperative for this team to collaborate closely with the research team.

Design Team

This team will be responsible for designing the layout for all of the information that we post publicly. Members of this team should have an understanding of graphic design and trends on social media sites. This group will work in conjunction with all teams. Also, this team should be aware of what content is being created and where it would garner the most engagements and reach. Finally, this team will have to be organized and use various digital tools to collect and organize data.

Expectations per Individual

Each student will share a Google doc with me. This doc will be a daily log of what you accomplish in class. This doc will be graded and a major part of your class participation grade and overall grade. You can do this on a Google doc or if you feel a Google spreadsheet would work better, you can use that option. It should include, but not limited to…

- brainstorming ideas
- tasks completed
- questions raised
- timeline for your work

Grading Notes…

You will be graded on your interaction and engagement with your team. This documentation will be the bulk of your grade. The end result will speak for itself. I am more interested in the process, your interaction with each other each day in class, and how you accomplish a task as a team.

What you should show and present at the conclusion of this project…

1. Utilize a digital or social media platform (subject to approval before account creation) to display your findings, research, and media content related to this topic. This medium will showcase your findings and serve as a resource for future [YOUR SCHOOL] students. You should include information you find, links, interviews, videos, pictures, etc. The media you post must be authored by you and cited properly.

2. Go to the source: Interview students, teachers, parents, and administrators and ask them what they know about digital citizenship and maintaining their digital identity. All interviews must have consent and message that this information will be posted online publicly. **NOTE: You may want to seek out a generic consent form.**

3. Submit research and studies that detail why it is imperative to maintain and understand your digital identity. This can come in the form of interviews

with teachers, administrators, experts, or articles you find online. Any assertion you make must include supporting evidence.

4. Cover all the bases: Think about what sites your peers use and find out all the good, the bad, and the ugly concerning these sites. *Example*: Find examples of students your age using social media or digital tools to promote positive change in the world or solve a problem.

5. Many say that Burlington High School (BHS) is crazy for allowing students to use iPads and mobile phones in class. Detail examples of what we are doing and why we are doing it. Provide examples in the form of research and studies as to why we allow these devices. Also, poll teachers and administrators. Seek out opportunities via Skype where we could connect with other schools to see what their perceptions are of BHS and our iPad initiative.

Timeline

I want the project managers to propose a working time frame for completing this project. Once submitted, we will stick to that schedule. If we need to adjust the schedule, the project managers must connect with me and provide support for extending the time.

So, what do you need to do in the next few classes...

1. Organize – Much like a project team would organize at, say Google, you want to organize organically and put the best people in the best places based on their skill sets. Each team should have a Google doc for their weekly schedule, agenda, and completed tasks. (Each student should share an individual Google doc with me and update daily.) This work will be a crucial part of your grade.

2. Space – Where are we going to house our information? Seek out the best space and find the best people to

work on the design. You'll want to seek out examples of other websites that present this topic.

3. Workflow – How will your team organize and communicate effectively to ensure that the project is on task and that everyone is working in an equitable manner?

4. Promote – How will you leverage social media and/or digital tools to promote and gain reach about the positive ways students are using social media?

This project did not click into motion right from the beginning. In fact, students were not really sure how to engage with a single objective and work together for a common goal. Plus, the subversive lesson in all this was that we need each other in order to complete the challenge and inevitably get a good grade. In one version of this, I didn't give them a rubric, but I also shared a rubric below.

The other piece of this that was unorthodox was that I did not provide a specific rubric for grading. I didn't want students working toward a grade, but rather, working toward a common goal. Life is about challenges and adapting to and solving them in the most efficient and economical means possible. Therefore, this type of assignment does not require a product to demonstrate the goal. It requires students to think, question, analyze, debate, and explore the most efficient, creative solution with the resources available to them. This is how our global economy functions and the employees with these skill sets are the ones they want to hire.

Building meaningful, offline relationships is essential to engaging in digital spaces. Students must understand that a friend is not simply a button you click to accept and that a conversation is not always typed into a small box. Technology can do great things for our lives and bring us all closer together; however, it shouldn't isolate us from personal relationships.

Student name:

Presentation Topic:

	100–85	84–70	69 – come on, really?
Understanding	The students demonstrate a clear understanding of digital citizenship, maintaining a responsible digital identity and creative commons use. The team explains why digital citizenship is imperative for students to understand and identifies specific examples of proper and improper use for support.	The students demonstrate a clear understanding of digital citizenship, maintaining a responsible digital identity and creative commons use; however, they fall short on providing support for their assertions and don't really clarify why it is important.	The students demonstrate a thin understanding of digital citizenship, maintaining a responsible digital identity and creative commons use. Support is thin and unclear.
Creating and illustrating	The students illustrate examples of digital citizenship and creative commons use through content they created, analyzed, and interpreted from the web. Students present support for their work and why it is important. All acquired content is cited properly.	The students illustrate examples of digital citizenship and creative commons use through content they created, analyzed, and interpreted from the web, but their content is scattered and unorganized. Citations are thin and present errors.	The students hardly illustrate examples of digital citizenship and creative commons use through content they created or analyzed and interpreted from the web. Students present no support or citations of their work.
Applying, evaluating, and presenting	Students present an engaging talk on their subject. Their presentation is interactive, clear, and engaging with the audience. Every member plays an important role in this group and demonstrates competency in all areas of digital citizenship and creative commons.	Students present a moderately engaging talk on their subject. Their presentation is clear but not engaging or interactive. It is clear that some members have stronger understanding than others.	Students' presentation is thin and unorganized. There is no central theme or message in the talk. It is clear that all members did not work collaboratively.

Teacher Narrative:

Classroom Activity: Social Media PSA

Objective:

Create a storyboard and a short 30-second to 1-minute Public Service announcement warning your peers against the dangers of social media use.

Guiding question:

What should students understand about social media use?

◆ This can cover any social media outlet: Facebook, Twitter, Instagram, etc.
◆ What should students be aware of when using social media? What are potential infractions? What are the consequences if used irresponsibly?
◆ Subjects to consider…

- Texting while driving
- Facebook/Twitter privacy
- Cyberbullying
- Using Twitter inappropriately
- Maintaining your digital identity
- Posting on Instagram

Expectations:

1. Develop a storyboard that outlines your PSA. This should be done on a Google doc that you share with me. This should roughly explain each shot of your video and how you intend the final product to look.
2. If you need to do any filming, it can be done on the iPad. Screencasts can use Jing. And editing should be done through iMovie. Music is not required but may be used in some instances.

Grading:

25% Storyboard – How well did you outline this project? Is it thorough and clear? Is the storyboard consistent with the final project?

25% Engagement (participation within group and class) – How well did you utilize your class time? Did you spend time in class distracted by games?

25% Editing – How well did you edit your video? Do your shots each have a purpose? Does the music fit? Are all media creative commons licensed? Did you cite your media?

25% Message – How well does your video convey your message? Is the message clear and concise? Is your story consistent with your storyboard? Is your message easy to understand?

We will watch the PSA videos on Thursday.

While educators and parents can make the best efforts to educate our students on digital health and wellness skills, we know that some may slip through the cracks. You can tell a classroom of 30 students to always look both ways before crossing the street, and one out of that 30 will always run without looking. In my experience creating and teaching a digital literacy course, I've seen this come true too many times. My point here is that we must continue our mission of educating students, not solely on academic merits but on ethical merits as well. Promote and model good uses of digital spaces in your classroom and school. Building a culture of digital health and wellness across a school district will ensure that our students carry out the missions posted on our walls.

5

Define Your Balance

Topics Covered in This Chapter:
- ♦ Finding a Balance in the Classroom
- ♦ Finding a Balance between Home and School
- ♦ A Day in the Life
- ♦ Mornings

The goal of this book is to help us all find balance with our access to digital avenues. While it may seem like I am trying to get you to quit smoking cold turkey, I am not. What I am trying to share is my experience over the last six years and what I noticed along the way. Things changed in our world and our society. I harken to the alternate future in *Back to the Future 2* when Biff Tannen is a billionaire, and all seems wrong with the world. As a society, we have been through a lot since 2016. It's when the lovely streets of Twitter, Facebook, and Instagram changed from a pleasant place to engage to an angry cauldron of shouting and anger.

This chapter is not about finding the good old days of social media but about finding a healthy balance of technology use in our lives as it exists today and where it is going. As I mentioned in Chapter 5, I took myself away from Facebook and solely use that application to see what everyone was doing. I have unfollowed many people who still use the forum to spread misinformation, hate, and conspiracy theories that just are not true. I use Twitter

DOI: 10.4324/9781003301325-6

in a completely new way than when I first joined in 2008. I follow my favorite Philly sportswriters and athletes and make lists for them. When I watch a game, I tend to follow those lists to check in on information about the game and what I may miss in the broadcast. Instagram and TikTok are where I spend most of my time these days. On Instagram, I post an occasional picture and story. TikTok I mostly observe and follow. I find both mediums highly engaging and simplistic in their design, allowing me to waste countless hours on each. And all this has happened within the last several years. As I mentioned earlier, much of this change came with the 2020 election and the aftermath, the global pandemic, and the murder of George Floyd. These events caused me to reflect and examine how I engage and use social media.

Finding a Balance in the Classroom

When I was in the classroom teaching about technology and working with teachers, students, and parents on these topics, the primary concerns were around how much time suffice for online activity and how should students at different ages begin to gain access to technology. My statement then as it is today (with a twist) was find the right balance. This should be the case with anything we do. When I was growing up, it wasn't the Internet that had my attention; it was my NES or Nintendo Entertainment System. I was hooked on Zelda and Super Mario Brothers and finding ways to advance and move to the next level in both games. Much like the generation before me with the TV, my parents, along with many parents, were convinced that this level of screen time would surely rot my brain. I can confirm my brain has not rotted. But, my parents did understand that I needed a balance between my screen time and how I engaged with video games. If it were left up to me, I surely would have played them anytime I wasn't at school, thinking about the video game and connecting with my friends on what level they achieved on the Legend of Zelda.

The same is true today regarding screen time; however, the game has changed significantly since I was a kid playing video games. And so have classrooms. When we look at the way social media has evolved, it has become, as I mentioned before, a mood-altering drug that 80% of the population takes 12 times a day. When you apply that metric to the current educational system and tack on the aftermath of a global pandemic that forced all of us drop any idea of balance for simply getting through the day.

When it comes to the classroom, the key to all of this is good instructional design, along with a consistent vision and culture built by the school administration. Find applications that promote and strengthen various skill sets for students, not just one or two. Look at applications that promote organization and workflow skills. Getting caught up in the never-ending, always expanding world of applications will only confuse your students and, inevitably, frustrate you.

There is an important scene in the movie *Hoosiers* during the team's first practice. The coach, played by Gene Hackman, walks into the gym and gathers the team together. He tells his team that practice is going to be different than what they are used to. The montage that follows highlights fundamental basketball. The boys are engaged in agility drills, ball handling drills, and a variety of defensive drills. Throughout the montage, you hear players asking when they are going to shoot and scrimmage. Hackman replies, "There's more to the game than shooting! There's fundamentals and defense."

While students and teachers alike are anxious to integrate new learning tools into the classroom, we must err on the side of caution. It is our responsibility to empower our students by giving them the fundamental lessons in digital citizenship. Like basketball, students must enter the world of social media and digital media with a good defense. They must understand the repercussions of irresponsibly using social and digital media and what effects it may have on their future. Give students time to use the device, but make sure they understand that the device is an outlet to many new avenues.

> Like basketball, students must enter the world of social media and digital media with a good defense.

Quick Tip for Teachers

Each year, before my students arrived, I would design my workflows in my classroom. Typically, this involved using the Learning Management System as our hub for two-way communication between me and my students. This was not only our town square but also our 1:1 connection. From there, I focused on core applications I would use in my classroom for that year. Essentially, what I was creating was the plumbing for my classroom. Information needed pipelines and access throughout the year. For example:

1. Our communication hub: Canvas LMS
2. Email was to be used: Only in an instance when the LMS was down or not working
3. Core classroom applications to teach and share:
   a) Explain Everything app – Dynamic presentation skills
   b) Google Slides – collaborative presentation and note taking skills
   c) Google Drive – organizational skills

And that's it. I would commit to using these tools throughout the year and also embedding them in projects. For example, I would teach students all the features of Google Slides by embedding these features in a lesson.
https://docs.google.com/presentation/d/101B78Oirrg LBfcfJ6eeGSFebwmE2ufvGNowGy6jIipE/edit#slide=id.p6
Additionally, this focus would not only help organize my entire class for me, as the teacher, but also organize my students.

As an administrator, seek to promote a culture of sharing around technology along with a pace that is comfortable for every level of user. Reinforce the idea that learning goals and objectives – not devices or applications – still drive classroom engagement. An administrator's biggest mistake is to make technology seem like a mandated item. Also, be sure your staff understands that a classroom technology misstep does not mean a negative evaluation. Rather, see it as a step in the learning process.

While making sure students are using technology appropriately and purposefully, it's important that technology departments ensure that faculty are supported throughout the year. In my experience, I have implemented a variety of strategies for making sure faculty and staff feel supported with the technology we offer at the school. In one instance, I implemented a "Genius Bar" concept every Thursday and rotated different schools each week. Initially, we had an open forum for questions and support. After the first few sessions, the team decided to provide focused sessions each week. Initially, the tech team members ran these sessions. We eventually had teachers and administrators asking if they could present as well. This was a great transition for everyone and helped expand the collective voice and mission of tech integration. This example also was geared to create ambassadors for technology and helped the tech team in supporting faculty, staff, and parents more broadly.

In addition to our Thursday Genius Bar, we created EdTech "Flashmobs" at a different school each week. We did not integrate a song or dance, but we organized as many members of the tech team as possible on one day and spread ourselves throughout that school. We visited classrooms, held drop-in sessions for teachers and students, and simply presented ourselves for any kind of help needed throughout any given day. In addition, this gave the tech team a good gauge on what schools needed with regard to tech and helped address any outstanding issues.

Administrators or department chairs should contemplate establishing uniform communication modules and essential applications for use by the team or the entire school. Ultimately, this comes down to equity for students and ensures they are not navigating to different applications for each of their classes throughout the day. In many cases, when I have talked to students, they prefer a consistent set of tools and workflows to better organize their classes and each day. I highly recommend that schools have these discussions as a community and design the workflows that all can commit to. This is not to say you cannot use or embed other applications, but when trying to strike a healthy balance for screen usage for both you and your students, it's best to be consistent and efficient.

Before we rush to judgment on technology integration as another sweeping phase in education, we should focus on finding a healthy balance for integrating technology in our respective classrooms. Ignore the clutter of overzealous EdTech enthusiasts and find your focus on designing your own instruction. Ultimately, it's not about how many apps we integrate but about providing our students with the best access and opportunities to contemporary learning resources. As educators, we must prepare our students for their future, not ours.

> As educators, we must prepare our students for their future, not ours.

Finding a Balance between Home and School

At the outset of the pandemic, schools across the world raced to get technology in the hands of their students so that they could access school at home during the quarantine period. What was fascinating about this time was the careless speed at which schools sent devices home. For years, schools spent resources on programming that focused on screen time and implemented pro-gramming that limited technology use while in school. And in an instant, all that changed and screens were going home without any hesitation.

Throughout my career, the balance of technology between home and school has always been difficult to traverse. Early in the book, I mentioned how having all devices under the same roof allowed us to manage and control a host of ways in which our users engaged with screens. But, when those screens went home, we were really at a loss for what we can control. And, despite the numerous software platforms out there that help parents manage and control the content and add filters to their kids devices, this is not a guarantee in every house and what's more is without parameters and norms for technology at home, even the best software will fall short of success.

As soon as a school begins introducing devices to students, parents must be involved in the conversation. This is not to say that parents have an open forum to decide school policy, but instead, present resources and training (will share shortly) on how the devices will be used in class, what applications students will have access to, and how students' data is protected. Once you have laid the groundwork for your technology policies, make sure you go over the acceptable use policy with them. In many cases, it's appropriate to have the parents and students sign this policy together. As I mentioned earlier, make sure you go over this with students in school and then provide some guiding questions for parents to go over when the students take this document home for parents to sign.

 ## Classroom Activity (for Home, Too)

The first step in creating a healthy balance of technology use is establishing norms both in school and working with parents to ensure there are norms and parameters around technology use when the devices are sent home. In the past, I have worked to create an acceptable use policy and make it digestible, inter-pretable, and actionable. Additionally, I changed the title from acceptable use policy to empowered digital use policy. We don't want students' first interaction with technology to be a negative one. Here is an example of what I mean:

EMPOWERED DIGITAL USE POLICY

The mission of [SCHOOL'S NAME] Educational Technology Office is to prepare and inspire all students to contribute and excel in a connected, global community responsibly. [SCHOOL'S NAME] provides engaging instruction that develops digital citizenship skill sets for using technology as a tool to achieve this mission. Information and digital literacy are an integral part of the [SCHOOL'S NAME] curriculum across all subjects and grades in developmentally appropriate ways. All students have access to a robust Wi-Fi network, current hardware, and applications to support learning and instruction.

I understand that using connected digital devices (whether personal or school owned) and the [SCHOOL'S NAME] network is a privilege. When I use them according to the Empowered Digital Use Guidelines, I will keep that privilege.

All members of the [SCHOOL'S NAME] community agree to follow the [SCHOOL'S NAME] Student Handbook and school rules and commit to the following Empowered Digital Use Guidelines.

I will:

- *Use digital devices, networks, and software in school for educational purposes and activities.*
- *Keep my personal information (including home/mobile phone number, mailing address, and user password) and that of others private.*
- *Show respect for myself and others when using technology, including social media.*
- *Give acknowledgment to others for their ideas and work.*
- *Report inappropriate use of technology immediately.*

Failure to respect the tenets of this policy will result in disciplinary action that aligns with the [SCHOOL'S NAME] Student Handbook Code of Conduct. [SCHOOL'S NAME] adheres to all Federal policies that include the Children's Internet Protection Act (CIPA). It provides provisions and filtering of all Internet content under the Federal Communications Commission (FCC) policies.

This policy is simple and easy to interpret and act upon. In many cases, I have read through school's acceptable use policies and while I understand what it all means, most students have no idea what is being asked of them. The document is signed at the beginning of the year and then that's it. However, I like to go over this document with students in class first and then send it home with students and present some guiding questions for them to go over with their parents.

1. How can I, the student, practice these same policies at home?
2. Should we add any policies to this document for technology use at home?
3. How should we decide how much time I can have on the screen after school?

Outcomes: With this activity, you are striking the balance between technology use at home and at school while ensuring that kids have a voice in this policy. Since I was a kid, I always disliked rules for rules sake and typically tried to break those or subvert them at any chance I could. However, when I had a voice in the process, all that changed and I wanted to stick to these rules since I had a part in creating them. In a sense, I had some pride and ownership of the rules. And this is what we want to get across when we are trying to create balance with technology use. Creating a balance does not mean redacting access, but rather, empowering the user with technology, but giving them voice in the process.

Once you have established a set of ground rules for balancing technology at home, you'll want to find times to engage parents in programming around a variety of topics. In many of the places I have taught and worked, I tried to create consistent programming that would invite parents in for a workshop or presentation on a trending topic or an emerging technology tool that we might be using. In 2011, while I was working at Burlington High School in Burlington, MA, we launched a 1:1 iPad initiative that Summer. We intentionally had students and parents sign up for hour long sessions in the Summer. Parents needed to accompany their child in order to get their iPad. Parents and kids arrived, they picked up their iPads, and then we walked them through the setup and getting them on WiFi. We also detailed our norms and use cases that we would be establishing throughout the year.

These sessions would not have been the same if we had not included parents in the process. Many parents during these sessions asked us a host of questions and continually asked how they could manage their network access at home. The important pieces of this simple event was to create transparency around our technology program, and ultimately, support parents with a device that was being provided by the school and eventually would come in to their homes. In today's connected world of home and school, most Internet service providers have upped their controls for parents so that parents can manage screen time and content that their kids are seeing easily.

Technology rollouts and initiatives should always be a community experience. While working in several schools, my tech team created several forums throughout the school year for both teachers and parents to get support on technology initiatives that were happening and proposed for future consideration. Every Tuesday, my tech team held weekly "How do I do That?" sessions at a different school. Initially, these sessions offered teachers a place to come after hours or during common time and get assistance with technology and ask questions. It's a very simple way of engaging both teachers and parents for tech support. Today, my team and I will run similar offerings via Zoom for parents and teachers. We can also record these sessions and send out to departments and parents in the event they cannot access the live session.

Another tech team I worked with held monthly "community tech nights." The purpose of these monthly sessions was to educate the community and parents on what technology students have access to, as well as trending topics around parenting in the digital age. Initially, we focused our sessions on what students were using. For example, we launched several new initiatives at the beginning of the 2017–2018 school year. One of the biggest transitions was to Google Apps for Education. This suite of apps was launched to our entire staff and student populations. For the first time in our district, students had email accounts K-12. The first conversation session we had with parents focused on what students had access to and what they could do with their new accounts.

As these Community Tech Nights evolved, we started working with our parent groups to find topics that appealed to them. While we continued to cover the applications and resources kids were using daily in school, we also started engaging speakers on these topics and having panel discussions with parents. One evening, we watched the movie, *Screenagers* and held a panel discussion after the movie. It was a great way to connect and share with parents and ultimately led to further sessions on ways we could connect with parents around technology use at school and at home.

After the viewing of the *Screenagers* movie, we held an in-person session on some of the questions and topics that came out of watching the movie *Screenagers*. This session was focused on digital health and wellness and helped further the partnership with technology and parents. After taking parents through a brief presentation on how we are supporting purposeful use of technology at school, I had the parents go through a few scenarios that got them talking about how each of them dealt with technology issues at home. Below is an example of what I did with parents.

 Activity for Parents

Anytime I present to parents, I like to engage them in a way that has them sharing best practices with other parents. I tend not to talk too much at them but will outline what we are doing in school or how we are teaching best practices around technology use in school and then get them talking to each other in small groups.

This is a session I like to call, "How do you deal?" It presents several scenarios to parents and asks them to share how they deal with each of the technology at home-centered scenario. Here's how it works with the scenarios:

1. Have parents huddle in small groups (more than two).
2. On a slide deck or a handout, present the scenarios.

3. Parents discuss each scenario and share how they deal with each scenario or what policies or rules they employ at home around technology use.
4. Groups will write down what they do for each scenario and share with the larger group.
5. Once everyone shares, in the second iteration, I have parents in those groups create a scenario within that group and share how they deal with it.

Here are some example scenarios I have used in the past:

Scenario 1: Your son or daughter comes home from school. They enter the house and go straight to their room and close the door. Their school laptop is in their backpack with them.

Scenario 2: It's dinner time and your son or daughter has their phone with them at the table. They are not using it, but it is placed next to their place setting.

Scenario 3: Your son or daughter asks for an increase in their data plan on their smartphone.

Outcomes of This Activity

The best outcome of this activity is getting parents talking to and sharing with each other about best practices for technology use at home. In some cases, parents have created a resource that they can all use, a Google sheet, for instance, that houses all of their ideas for best practices for technology use at home. In one example of running this presentation, I had parents come up with a list of solutions for some of the scenarios that were presented. Here is what that list looked like:

◆ Designate a common area charging station in home.
◆ Setup a guest network account on home WiFi for parents and students.
◆ Buy kids an alarm clock.
◆ Designate one night a week for non-digital family activity.
◆ Model active, purposeful use of technology.

Ultimately, the goal here is to present parents with resources and support when their kids are at the youngest ages. As a technology leader in your school, be part of the solution and the conversation every chance you get. In my experience, I have found that transparency and healthy communication between home and school around technology will go a long way with parents. The goal is never to create the rules or parameters for them but provide them with the resources and support so they can effectively implement their own guidelines for their kids at home. Plus, in many cases, I have seen parents creating their own groups and chat threads through text or Slack to continually connect and collaborate on technology use at home. When it comes to the relationship between technology use at home and at school, ongoing, consistent conversation is key to really supporting our kids and ensuring that they are experiencing a healthy amount of screen time at home and at school.

A Day in the Life

When I set out to write this book, I didn't want it to sound preachy but instead offer ideas that I have used in the past to meet the demands of the shifting culture around digital tools and human engagement. A few of the motivators for this book were the 2016 election, the global pandemic, and a podcast called *Offline* with Jon Favreau. All of these things, coupled with my own shifting experience with Facebook, Twitter, Instagram, etc. And, what I hope readers take from this book are strategies and anecdotes for their own, shifting digital mindset. We are at a tipping point with a lot of these tools that many of us really couldn't quite foresee coming to fruition. But, now we are here and we must adjust.

In many cases, these tools have increased the temperature on hate speech and general anger toward each other. In our country, we seem so divided. And this is not the first time we had stark divisions in our country. The Civil War being the most memorable. But, do you think the Civil War would have ever ended had there been access to the Internet and digital tools we have today?

It's hard to tell, but fascinating to imagine what could have happened in the presence of these tools. This is why we must shift the way we teach digital tools in school, shift our digital mindset, and ensure our kids know how to effectively navigate digital tools and worlds.

I have shared ways in which we can audit our daily lives, set goals for ourselves, hold ourselves accountable, and find a balance with technology and our lives. But, what does this all look like in action day to day? Many of us need to use technology as part of our work lives; students use it for many engagements throughout their school day. In this section, I am going to walk you through my digital day. I will be honest and share current trends with my digital life and how I plan on evolving it moving forward. I want the readers of this book to understand I am not just researching these topics but also living them.

Mornings

To begin, as I am writing this sentence, I have my phone next to me and am wearing an Apple watch. I have both devices set to "Do Not Disturb" which will silence all haptics and sounds coming through. But, before I get there, let's start in the morning. Let's begin with Monday morning. Next to my bed, I have my iPhone and Apple watch charging next to me. I have an Alexa clock on my bedside nightstand as well. I use the Amazon Echo Spot as my alarm clock and when I wake up, I ask it the weather. Unfortunately, one of my bad habits that I told you I would be honest about in this segment is taking my phone off the charging pad and the scrolling begins. I check muted notifications that occurred over night. Who texted, check email, quick scroll through Instagram. Double tap for a quick like. Wait, what did I just like? Who cares. This occurs for way to long and something I am working on fixing in the coming year.

When it comes to my morning, I have a few points of feedback for myself and anyone else who can relate to morning scrolls through utter nonsense. When I step back for a moment and look at myself lying there next to my wife, both of us silent and scrolling on our phones, what I reflect on is that during most of these morning sessions, I have gained zero from it in my life. In fact, I have probably decreased cognition and possibly created unneeded anxiety for myself before my feet even touch the bedroom floor. This is also the case for many of our students. Most of us will admit to sleeping next to our phones and checking in with them at all times of the night, before bed, and first thing in the morning. It's not great. In fact, many of our students have no idea what it feels like to wake to a piercing, analog alarm clock. The easy solution here and something I mentioned earlier is to get an alarm clock for yourself and charge your phone in another room. Problem solved. When you go up to bed, place your phone on a charger in another room, tuck it in, and say goodnight. In place of aimlessly scrolling, try reading a book, a magazine, or something not scrollable and analog. Whatever your solution, tuck your phone in and get out of bed to find it in the morning.

As I am getting ready, my phone is typically by my side. And yes, like many of us, the phone comes to the bathroom with me. I recently came upon an article in *The Washington Post* titled, "We all use phones on the toilet, just don't sit more than 10 minutes." As I have been writing this book, the amount of pertinent articles I have stumbled upon have been numerous. This one struck particularly interesting. In the article, it's mentioned that there are two types of people in the world: people who check their phone in the bathroom and those who lie about checking their phone in the bathroom. And, if you have worked in the school, you know this is going on day to day. I bring this point up because the doctors in this article stress the following:

Which prompted the question: Is it healthy to sit on the toilet with a phone? I turned to a gastroenterologist for answers.

"You generally don't want to spend more than about on average about 10 minutes," said Dr. Roshini Raj, a gastroenterologist at NYU Langone, and the author of "Gut Renovation," a book about digestive health. Though Raj acknowledged that — like with many things in medicine — there's not a one size

fits all answer, she pointed to three potential pain points for preoccupied poopers.

(Klimentov, 2022)

I won't get into the pain points listed because this is not a book about digestive health. But, you get my point. Much like when we go to bed, we leave the phone out of the bathroom. Regardless of the time spent with phone in bathroom, just think of all the opportunities for the spread of germs.

That's how I typically spend my mornings with technology present for most of it. Maybe as you are reading this, you are relating to it as well, or maybe you are much better than I am and have these strategies in place. Again, think about children at the youngest age and how much of a sponge they are for everything that adults do and say. Technology has a big place in this. If you sleep next to your phone every night and spend hours with it in the bathroom, it's most likely that your kids will eventually take on these habits.

The Work Day

This section is hard to write because we all have different ways in which our jobs dictate how much or how little we engage with technology daily. But, what I hope to share is my experience and some of the workflows that have worked for me both working in the classroom and as a school administrator. Additionally, I want to share how technology fits into our home. Right now, it's just my wife and I, but when we have children, I want to begin planning how we will incorporate technology into their life and ensure we guide them with the right tools and skills.

At work, I have a rule, if it's an email, I usually will respond within a day and don't treat the message as urgent or something I need to attend to immediately. With this norm in place, I like to block out an hour in my day and read my emails. This hour is never first thing in the morning, but rather sometime in the afternoon or early evening. I found in the past reading emails first thing in the morning would disrupt the flow of my day and I felt less productive. I would come up from air after reading through and responding to emails and realize I hadn't even read my to do list. Speaking of to do lists, I like to keep one daily. There are a host of options I have tried for this and have come to a conclusion, digital to do apps require a commitment and a consistent workflow. I have had the same experience with macro nutrient tracking. In the beginning, you are on top of it and logging information daily at each meal. As time goes on, these habits wane and it's easy to get off track. The reason? In my estimate, it's because I am adding items to a to do list on a device that has so many other avenues to distract. In many cases, I have had colleagues reach out and ask me what I use for to do list apps or productivity tools. And my answer is always the same, you gotta test drive them all and find out what is right for you. What is best for you might not be an app, it may very well be a pen and paper.

I have tried a pro version of Asana, Tick Tick, Evernote, Google Keep, Things App, Google Tasks, and Apple Reminders. I gave each application a run through for several months and tested out all the capabilities before removing it from my phone and my workflow. I will not be sharing a detailed experience of any particular app or endorsing any of them, but what I found is that there is no perfect app for me. But, what I use daily to manage my day to day and allows me the least amount of screen time with that particular application is Apple Reminders and Notes. What I like about both of these native iPhone tools is that I can use my voice to add reminders whether I am in the car, or walking around without my phone and only my Apple watch to serve me. I use the Reminders app at both work and in my personal life. My wife and I have shared lists for groceries and our bills. This allows us for seamless communication via a single app that limits our screen time and keeps us informed when we're together or traveling.

At work, I use Reminders and Notes for my meetings and day to day. In many cases, I have to walk into a classroom and assess a projector unit, for example, that is not working. With the Notes app, I can take pictures, make notes in line, and create a reminder for when this is due and needs to be replaced. I can also share this note among all my devices. It's easy for me and has been the most productive way for me to work. This is not to say it will work for you, but as I mentioned before, give all of these tools a try. What I like about both the Reminders app and the Notes app is that they are both boring. The design is function over form. For that, it helps me focus and get things done. In the classroom, we should consider the same thing when designing workflows for students. Think about the distraction factor and the options on the periphery.

 Classroom Activity

When thinking about day to day with technology in the classroom, I always made sure I included student voice in the process. In many cases, I found myself learning from them when they shared different applications they used and workflows they organically used to manage their classes and day to day. A great week 1 activity for students, that can be implemented across all content areas and grade levels, is to have a Shark Tank style presentation of productivity applications.

1. This can be done with partners, groups, or individually.
2. Present a host of applications that you have reviewed with your tech department or have students submit applications that they would like to use and then review with tech to ensure data privacy and applications work within the environment.
3. Students will spend time using the apps for class for a few days. Then, students present Shark Tank pitches to the class. (Teachers can choose to create a rubric for evaluation or simply hold a vote based on the presentation.)
4. Students will vote on the app they wish to invest their time and energy in throughout the year.
5. At the end of the year or the semester or unit, have students review their experience using the applications in class. Is it something the class should continue using? Or do we need to pivot?

Outcomes

What I love about this activity from the outset is that it establishes community in the classroom immediately. It gets students evaluating workflows and using critical thinking skills to see what works best for them and ultimately each other. It sets the tone that student voice will be at the forefront of decisions and ideas to make the class more inclusive of all voices and reinforces presentation and strong communication skills. And, while this outcome doesn't quite fit into the Universal Design for Learning or UDL, you may need to make accommodations for students to support their learning style.

Beyond the work day, I will admit that in my personal life throughout any given day, I have a lot of bad habits with my phone. These habits are currently under review in my head as I approach the new year and the launch of this book. And, I am sure many of you out there are thinking the same thing about your digital habits. However, as I mentioned earlier in this book, I started evaluating my social media presence after the 2020 election. When it was all said and done, I stepped back from my phone and how I was using many of the applications on it and did a hard reflection on my actions and what I was gaining from everything I was sharing and engaging with daily. I found that I was angrier than usual, and most of my engagements centered around trying to get a dig in at someone or prove "the other side" wrong. I was engaging in random conversations with strangers about political beliefs and pushing arguments that would never have a real winner or loser.

I centered a lot of my reflection on how I was spending my time and what I was gaining from these interactions. When I scrolled back through online arguments on Facebook or Instagram, I came to the conclusion that what I was doing was an utter waste of time and that I was yielding zero gains from any of it. Posting an article, hoping to get a rise or reaction from the "other side" accomplished zero in my efforts. I was not going to magically convert someone to my way of thinking by posting an article that I thought made my point. Or, engaging and commenting on other's posts that I thought would change their mind and prove a point. Again, zero return on investment. This is when I decided to live the last few chapters that I just shared with you and do a complete audit of how I engage with and use social media and digital tools.

As I set out to audit my digital life, I needed to focus on the applications I was using most and spending the most time with. Anyone who knows how social media companies work, will know that my bad habits feed into their algorithms and increase engagement. I was "doom scrolling" far too much and hooked into seeing and liking what everyone was doing. And then TikTok came into my life. Just as I was moving away from Facebook and all it stood for, in walks TikTok to take the place of an application I no longer engaged with. But, let me pause here for a minute. As I was auditing my digital life, I came to a few conclusions. Facebook was toxic and I needed to get away from it. I rarely used Snapchat but had an account, but did more consuming than creating. Instagram was a place I always enjoyed and hoped to live on this digital street for the long haul. Even though it's owned by META, I still liked the simplicity of it and that I could create stories that showcased me and my life and also engage and share with friends through a simple interface. TikTok came into my life more recently, but I only created a few of them and mostly used the app like I used YouTube ten years ago.

On my main screen are the primary apps that I use, and then if you swipe left, those are what I consider to be the secondary apps that I engage with or spend more time with, like the New York Times where I do my daily Wordle and Mini Crossword and the Boston Globe, which I read completely digitally. I also spend Sunday mornings with the New York Times print edition. During my Sunday morning routine of coffee and the analog New York Times, I try not to have my phone nearby. I focus my time on the paper and leave my phone in another room and if there are articles, I want to share with colleagues or friends, I will keep the paper open and share later.

Evenings

As much as I want to tell you and pretend like I am able to put my phone away when I get home from work, I do not. I find this time to be my most vulnerable for digital bad habits. On my way home, I typically listen to music or a podcast. I do the same on the way to work. And, I will be honest, I wasn't always the best digital citizen in my car. With the advancements of CarPlay from Apple, I have gotten better about not looking at my phone while driving. I say this and am honest about it, because I find it to be one of the worst outcomes of our connection to digital tools. When I was training for the Boston Marathon (humble brag) in 2018 and 2020, one thing I noticed while running on roads was the amount of times I saw someone with their head down while operating a vehicle that was driving a certain speed and could cause serious damage in an instant. I cannot stress enough how important this piece is. As we become more connected to our phones and what is on them, it infiltrates our lives in spaces that were not designed for them to be present. The car, crossing the street, the classroom, etc. When our heads are down into a screen and not paying attention in these scenarios present life-altering dangers to ourselves and those around us. Even on the way to and home from work, I glance at drivers passing me, and there is typically one hand on the wheel and one hand doing something on the phone. I cannot stress this enough, there are moments in our lives where our phones MUST be on the sidelines. The thought of injuring one's self or others at the cost of an arbitrary text or message is just not worth it.

When I arrive home from work, I will typically go to the gym, come home, and then begin to prepare dinner. In all of these endeavors, I do not need my phone. When my wife and I have dinner, our phones are present, but we are trying to keep them away from the dinner table. Especially when kids come into the picture, we will not have technology at the dinner table, nor will we use screens as a crutch to engage kids while they eat dinner. I know I am not yet a parent and I can imagine those of you that are parents that are reading this chapter are saying, "Just wait." But, I was not raised on screens, we had dinner and we talked as a family. We didn't have a TV in our kitchen until I was well into high school. Our entertainment during breakfast was the back of cereal boxes. Lunch was always a wild card, but dinner was sacred. Dinner we engaged with each other and spent time with each other. So to say there are no proof points for this working is false. All Boomers and GenXers had these experiences and now with their own kids and grandkids, they seem to be using the screen to solve a problem quickly, but it will only exacerbate the effects of the screen on a child.

As I mentioned earlier, most of my screen time happens in the evening after dinner, before bed, and in the morning. I also engage with my phone while I am watching sports games. I have created lists on Twitter of sports writers of my favorite teams and will follow along for insights and updates throughout the game. I like TikTok and find myself spending a lot of time aimlessly scrolling through videos of kids dancing or creating short skits that keep me engaged. All set to music that is quick and catchy. In my own personal life, this is where I need to get better. I need to set up time for myself to engage with these apps with a purpose and not just aimlessly scroll through arbitrary videos that don't add anything to my life.

My day in the life is certainly not yours. With this chapter, I wanted to be open, honest, and transparent not only about how I have restricted my digital life but also the work I still need to do. There is always work that needs to be done and it's good practice to stop and reflect occasionally and check in with yourself. What's more, it's a good practice for families to check in with each other and have conversations about their digital usage. I don't know how many times I am at a kids birthday party or out to dinner with my wife and when I look around I see people together spending more time with their phones than with the humans sitting in front of them. We accept it, we do it, but why? In my experience, I view this as a way to deal with social anxiety. When you are engaged with your phone, you are in a safe place that you have complete control over. When you take the phone away, you are you, and you have to be on in these settings. My worry in all of this is that we are changing our behaviors based on a device that gives us comfort.

In all of this, it's important to stop, pause, and reflect on your digital usage and how it affects you and those around you. My day in the life is not a prescription for success, but rather ideas and opportunities for each of us to reflect on our digital usage. That's what this entire book is supposed to be. It's not a prescription or an attack on your way of life with your phone, but rather a nudge to begin thinking about your digital mindset and how it impacts you and those around you.

Reference

Klimentov, M. (2022, November 30). "We all use phones on the toilet. Just don't sit more than 10 minutes." *The Washington Post* Retrieved December 9, 2022, from https://www.washingtonpost.com/video-games/2022/11/29/sitting-toilet-10-minutes-phone-nintendo-switch/

6

Be Accountable

Partner Up

Any time I set goals for myself, I like to have a partner to hold me to my timeline and my goal. In many cases, I have done weight loss challenges with colleagues and friends. The motivation of the group helps keep us all in check and ensure that we are holding each other accountable. However, my biggest success with this widely used strategy came in 2017–2018. In the Fall of 2017, I had some friends encourage me to run the Boston Marathon with them for Dana Farber. Now, I had been a casual runner up until this point and ran a few 5Ks, but the thought of running a full marathon never crossed my mind. But, I was in and started this journey in December of 2017.

I was very intimidated when I arrived to the first group run on a Saturday morning in December in Wellesley, MA. But, what I soon discovered was that I was surrounded by people just like me. No one here was running for the world marathon record;

DOI: 10.4324/9781003301325-7

rather, they were here to put in the work to support someone they knew who was battling cancer or who had passed on because of the cancer. As the training went on, I became more motivated and believed I could actually run a marathon. What kept me going were the friends I made within the Dana Farber team. We held each other accountable but also pushed each other and supported each other through the training. Ultimately, we all crossed the finish line in April 2018 and donated a lot of money to support cancer research.

The reason I bring up this story is because of the way we held each other accountable. If I had set out on my own to run a marathon, I might not have had the same results. That's not to say I don't believe in myself, but when you set out on a mission alone, it's easier to cheat or not give the full effort. When you have the support of a friend or a group, you have organic accountability structures built in. As the last part of this journey toward a better digital engagement, we must include others and hold each other accountable.

As I mentioned earlier, it was easy to remove my Facebook app off of my home screen so I am not continually checking it. But the challenge is creating sustainable workflows for our new habits of mind. And, This is a strategy that can work for both adults and students who are setting out on their pathway to becoming a good digital citizen. For adults, it is a check-in with ourselves and our accountability partner to examine what we hope to get out of achieving a new digital mindset. Below I will share ways in which both students and adults can begin this process and engage with a digital accountability partner.

> But the challenge is creating sustainable workflows for our new habits of mind.

Activity for Adults and Teachers

Set your goals: Think about how you engage with social media and your smartphone. List two goals that you would like to break and action steps and accountability metrics for each. (You can add more or less if you desire. Remember, this should be manageable and the goal is not to quit everything all at once, but rather to create sustainable habits with digital tools.) For example:

Goal	Action	Progress diary
I want to spend less time on my phone.	◆ I will set focus filters on my phone so that If I need my phone for work, I can just access those applications. ◆ I will turn off non-work notifications so that I am not inclined to pick up and use my phone without purpose. ◆ I will get an alarm clock and charge my phone in another room so that I am not inclined to scroll on my phone aimlessly before bed or first thing in the morning.	In this section, users would date each week and share how you have been achieving your goals. You could also share this portion with your accountability partner during check-ins.
I want to authentically and positively engage on social media when I am using it.	◆ When I am using social media, I will only post positive items with family and friends. ◆ I will refrain from engaging in comments that involve politics or controversial issues.	

What is shared here can be done with parent groups or teachers. Either way, it is great to model this first before sharing with students. As I have mentioned many times throughout this book, modeling is key, especially when we are dealing with elementary students who are very impressionable. When adults set the rules for technology use, they need to experience the same set of rules. If parents are observed by their children as constantly face down in a phone scrolling endlessly, parents cannot expect that these habits won't trickle down to their kids. The same with teachers. Teachers must model good use of technology and make sure that any recommendations I am sharing in this book are also done so by adults and children.

In the next section, I will share how accountability partners can be setup with students in your classroom. You can adapt these recommendations for different age levels. But, I recommend having conversations with your kids about technology use and what your goals as a family are before you send your kids off to school. It's a good practice to set up norms at home with your children and have conversations with neighbors and parents of kids who all go to the same school. Get on the same page as a school community and make sure you are supporting good digital habits before the bad ones form.

Hold Yourself Accountable

Several years ago, one of my recommendations to students and parents when discussing technology use both at school and at home was to turn off notifications. Eliminate the distractions, the dings, and the on-screen pop ups. I did this myself and soon noticed that I wasn't really missing out on anything of major importance. When I met with parents who struggled to know whether their kids were using the school-issued device for homework or playing games, I encouraged them to check-in with their son or daughter and have a conference at home about technology use. I recommended to both parents and students to turn their notifications off to a degree where they could still not only connect with communications and work but also set time aside in your day to check-in on "notifications."

Quick Tip: When technology comes home for the first time or at the beginning of each school year, have a conference with your children.

1. Set parameters for using the home WiFi.
2. Check in on the LMS or with the student planner to see how much homework is due.
3. Create a system when you can check in with notifications each day to keep up with communications.

If I were giving these recommendations today, I would have parents conference with their kids and look at the screen time statistics on their phone. This detailed data shows you how much screen time you engaged in each week, what applications you spent the most time on, and how many notifications you received. Additionally, there are parental controls that you can add to your child's device. These conversations are a must before giving kids the key to a really fast car with boundless avenues to drive. Also, use the driving analogy when introducing a smartphone with wireless and application access. With phones, like with cars, parents, guardians, and educators need to sit in the passenger side while kids are learning to drive.

> With phones, like with cars, parents, guardians, and educators need to sit in the passenger side while kids are learning to drive.

Personally, when I am looking to manage food control in my life, I use an application to track my food intake for the day. I track my food based on macro nutrients and stay within those parameters each day. It allows me to see patterns and learn from week to week how I am progressing in my goals. Prior to food tracking apps being readily available and designed in a way that made food tracking convenient, I used a small notebook to track my food. I would write down what I would eat throughout the day and track it in my note nook. I bring this up because much like learning to drive, we must take a paper test before we get to place our hands on the wheel.

 ## Classroom Activity

Objectives:

Students will be able to organize their digital engagements.
Students will be able create accountability metrics for each other.

1. Students are assigned or choose their digital accountability partner.

2. Students begin by assessing their day to day and how much time they should spend on social media applications (if 13+). If under 13, students can sub in video games, TV, or iPad time.
    a) Example: I would like to spend 30 minutes on my iPad after dinner each day.
    b) Example: I would like to spend 1 hour on screens after I have been active and outside on the weekend.
3. Students would have a notebook where they can write their goals down at the top of each page:
    a) EXAMPLE PAGE
        i.) Date Day of the week: April 1, 2023.
        ii.) Goal: I would like to spend 30 minutes on my iPad after dinner each day.
        iii.) Morning: *Students should log what they did in place of looking at screens.*
        iv.) Afternoon.
        v.) Evening: During my 30-minute window of screen time, I…
4. Once goals are set for each student, they will have class time to connect each week and share their experiences.

Before we redact, block, or hold students' access to devices, we need to implement an educational design that teaches students how to responsibly use these tools and create accountability metrics. I will go back to the driving analogy again. If you redacted access to driving resources, and just threw a kid into the driver's seat without any prior knowledge, what do you expect would happen? It's pretty clear. Also, these skills must be woven into the curricular fabric of every school. More often than not, we take the approach of blocking or redacting access for our students and don't touch the subject of digital health and wellness. Unfortunately, this is the case in most schools. These concepts and skills are seen as "computer class" topics and rarely make it into the content area subjects. Yet, students are exposed to and using a connected device almost every single day of their lives. Again, would you do the same with a car? I hope not.

These curricular conversations must start at the administrative level and ensure that teachers are trained and a part of these conversations. You wouldn't have a former engineer teach *Hamlet*, but if you provided that engineer with training and refined their skills with *Hamlet*, you would be better off. Schools must incorporate the same style of training or coaching within. The best part about working in a school is you have your experts in specific areas, but you also have broad spectrum of skills that teachers possess and are eager to share. This doesn't mean you have to send all of your teachers to a major conference to learn technology use skills; rather, leverage the expertise inhouse which I assure you is there.

Technology Must Be Like Oxygen

This final section of this chapter is sourced from a quote my dear friend and colleague, Chris Lehmann said around 2009, "Technology must be like oxygen: ubiquitous, necessary, and invisible." I would update this quote and add, continually assessed by the individual and those tasked with teaching technology skills. Chris always got it. He understood the potential for technology in schools but never focused on the tech, but rather the skills, but more importantly, the inquiry skills that students needed to thrive in the 21st century and beyond.

There is no denying that technology is omnipresent in our daily lives, but the majority of us reading this book lived in a time where this wasn't the case. We all grew up with a multitude of different distractions and technology that was supposed to rot our collective brains. These claims never really came to fruition. But, despite all of this, the game has changed dramatically for our students and ourselves as adults trying to lead young adults. As educators, we must adapt and adjust. If the pandemic taught us one thing, it is that the status quo is always poised to be upended. We must never inflict our past on the future of our students and children; rather, we should make strides to understand the technology of the time and seek ways in which we can prepare, support, and teach our students so that they have the skills and tools to solve the problems of tomorrow.

Preparing students for their future and not ours is one of the biggest takeaways I want readers to take from this book. Avoiding technology or assuming it does more harm than it does positive is not the right approach by this generation of adults and leaders. Rather, we must seek ways to understand our students' lives, the technology that is present and accessible to them, and understand and evaluate our own habits with technology and digital worlds. We must seek ways to bring technology into our classroom in purposeful, meaningful ways rather than shun its existence. And, while I will always argue the best technology in a classroom is a well-equipped, adaptable, empathetic teacher, that same teacher must provide guide rails on the technology in order to prevent bad habits from forming.

I run into former students more often than not. And one of the consistent pieces of feedback I get is "Marcinek, thanks for preparing me for what is really out there." This is by no means a stroke of my ego, but I taught skills not a specific content area the last time I was in the classroom. When I was teaching at Burlington Public Schools, I had the opportunity to teach a Digital Literacy course and a Student Help Desk course. Both of these courses focused on solving problems and designing support resources for a population of over 2,000 students and teachers. In both instances, they had not been done before. They were not in any school curriculum, but the students I had in these courses I made sure to follow up with over time. They have all done so well and have shared their recent successes with me. Most recently, I ran into a former student at a coffee shop near where I work. This former student's name is also Andy, and when I saw him, I asked him if he worked around this area. His response, "I actually work from here, my partner works at this coffee shop, and I work from my laptop here." I got my coffee and sat down with him for a few minutes. I was by far the least cool person in this coffee shop in Cambridge, MA, but I was happy to connect with one of my former students and see him thrive. I asked him if his experience in Burlington helped give him the grounding and skills to do the kind of work he is doing now. The answer was yes. He understood the potential and downside of technology. Still, he was poised to design and lead in these spaces based on the experience he had with technology and that it was seen as a positive and not something that was redacted or blocked from his education.

The wrap-up of this chapter is that technology use in all of our lives should be natural and necessary. Technology should be purposeful and meaningful in our lives and help us create new efficiencies in our day to day. The problem with many adopters of technology is that it is an outlet to a rabbit hole of more content that, for better or worse, is not needed in one's life. In all my experience with technology, I have always come back to Chris Lehmann's words. Technology must serve a purpose in my life and not just be something I consume blindly. Rather, technology must be a way to create and establish new efficiencies in my life. Period. End of story. This is what I have always believed and why I am on this journey to audit and evaluate my digital mindset and find more efficient ways in which I am using and connecting with others via technology.

> Technology should be purposeful and meaningful in our lives and help us create new efficiencies in our day to day.

Reference

Lehmann, C. (2009). "School tech should be like oxygen." *YouTube*. Retrieved December 9, 2022, from https://www.youtube.com/watch?v=RUWzQYLqLLg.

Afterword: Bringing It All Together

Throughout this book, there is one consistent theme, and that is balance. Not having balance in our life can create extreme frustration throughout our days. This is not to say that social media has no part in these frustrations; however, most of us who haven't found the right balance of social media use may find ourselves angrier than those who have found balance. Suppose we spend all of our days in a social, digital world chock-full of conspiracy theories. In that case, misinformation lies shouting, we're going to be an angrier population, and we're going to be more divided. My worry in all of this is if we don't balance things now, we may have a future in which we are constantly divided, we avoid connecting, and we don't socialize anymore.

This book is not meant to be a silver bullet and that once you read it, everything will be amazing again. It is meant to be less wordy and digestible so that it can be picked up and thought through in the moment. I want it to provide quick, actionable solutions that do not create more heavy lifts in our lives. We have a lot of work to do, and it starts with using the antidotes I've laid out in this book in both our own personal lives as adults and how we teach our students. If we as adults are not taking accountability for our use of social media and screen time on a day-to-day basis, then our students and our kids will continue to model our bad

> If we as adults are not taking accountability for our use of social media and screen time on a day-to-day basis, then our students and our kids will continue to model our bad habits.

DOI: 10.4324/9781003301325-8

habits. It starts with us the adult, the educator. We need to be responsible and not redact these subjects from our schools but instead embrace them each and every day. We need to give kids a roadmap and skill sets on how to manage and hold themselves accountable for their own actions within social media and their day-to-day lives.

Think about it this way. When a child is born, they are subject to a screen from the minute they are born. A picture is taken on a digital phone, and that image goes up to a cloud-based server where that child's image is stored and preserved for an infinite amount of time. Many kids have their images and social presence created before they can even open their eyes. We create digital profiles and footprints for our kids before they can fully understand the world they are brought into. This leads to the device being used to curb behavior, and eventually, the lure of the screen takes hold. The future of screen use begins and ends with us as adults.

If adults are injecting bad digital habits from day one of a child's life, it will only get worse unless we create norms and parameters. Again, I am not scolding parents for wanting to capture the precious, unforgettable moments in our lives, but rather take the time to reflect and understand what is happening when these digital worlds are opened up to kids at the youngest age. I don't have many pictures from the day I was born. There are a handful, maybe four or five total. There are the picture when I came home and me meeting my grandparents for the first time, but there is not this step-by-step timeline of the beginning of my life. And, quite frankly, I am fine with that. The generation before us had less technology to capture these moments. But, now we, and the generation born after the iPhone was launched, have a different set of opportunities to capture and share moments. It's almost as if in order to live an experience, we need to share it. It's a wild place we are in, but we have resources and opportunities to pause, reflect, and change our digital lives and mindset.

While the sharing and community aspect of social media has always been promising for our society, unfortunately, it has taken a dark turn. We must remind ourselves of these moments as we move forward in our lives. We possess the amazing

> We possess the amazing power to create these tools, but with great power comes great responsibility.

power to create these tools, but with great power comes great responsibility. It's up to adults and educators to educate us about these tools that ultimately our kids will inherit and have to govern and manage. We can no longer redact these tools within our schools or homes. And, instead of redacting, we must strive to put structures in place that bring technology to our students at the youngest age in a way that is purposeful and responsible. Taking something away or not introducing it does our students a disservice in their learning.

I will end this book with a personal story. I lost my Dad suddenly in 2017. He went to sleep and never woke up on March 19, 2017. My Dad never had an email address; he never had a cellphone or a mobile number. My Dad never sent a text in his life. My Dad didn't read a digital newspaper or magazine. When my Dad played fantasy football, he used the newspaper to add up his points. When I was growing up, I had a moment in my life which I will never forget. The moment was around 1995 when the Internet came into our house for the first time. I will never forget sitting in front of my home computer and watching the ESPN.com site unfold in front of my eyes. This experience triggered something in my mind, I suddenly knew more than my father in some regard. I could access information and resources that my Dad did not have. And while at the time I may have considered myself advanced and ahead of the game, I was completely wrong.

I may have had access to this new trove of information, but it wasn't about access, but rather what I was going to do with it. How would it propel me forward and support my learning and career going forward. Just because we have access to something, doesn't mean we can wield its potential in an instant. And this is where my Dad was right. He didn't use a cellphone because he didn't see the potential or use in his life. In his world, as long as he had family and friends around him and

> Just because we have access to something, doesn't mean we can wield its potential in an instant.

his newspaper and television, he could be informed and further educate himself. He watched me get an iPhone from day one and warned against its time suck and unproductive nature. In the moment, I thought my Dad was a fossil and a burgeoning Boomer who wanted to tramp down the next generation so he could still prove he was contemporary and engaged with his world. I have never been more wrong in my life. Much of this book is a silent homage to my father, who understand the power of books, analog media, and human engagement. Why did I need to see what everyone was doing each day all at once? Why did I need to engage in a forum that allowed everyone to talk about something all the time all at once? How were these forums and applications advancing society?

In their infancy, many of these tools and applications showed great promise. But, with anything, the downtown mainstreet feel to many social media applications soon turned to overcrowded spaces where everyone is shouting and no one is listening. They went from productive tools for sharing and advancing a message or our career to dumpsters of garbage that served very little outside of consuming information that may or may not be true and spreading conspiracy theories that trapped many into an endless spiral of lies and misinformation. When I was writing my first book, I was speaking much differently about these tools and social media. I will never forget how proud my Dad was when he held my book in his hands and how proud he was after reading it. He even started using the computer more often after reading it. In many ways, I wrote that book for him and wanted him to see the potential for the tools that were now constants in my daily life. When I set out to write this book, I knew he would never have a chance to read it. But, I wanted him to know that in many ways this book was about all the positive lessons my Dad instilled in me. It was a way of showing that he was right in a lot of his choices to not engage with digital tools and applications, and instead, live in the moment and savor every aspect of it. My Dad would rather be in the picture, than taking it or sharing it to social media. That's who he was. In my life, he was the last of his kind. It's hard to find someone like him anymore. Thank you, Dad. You really were ahead of your time.

For Product Safety Concerns and Information please contact our EU
representative GPSR@taylorandfrancis.com
Taylor & Francis Verlag GmbH, Kaufingerstraße 24, 80331 München, Germany

www.ingramcontent.com/pod-product-compliance
Ingram Content Group UK Ltd.
Pitfield, Milton Keynes, MK11 3LW, UK
UKHW021436080625
459435UK00011B/281